An AuDHD Memoir

A Raw Journey of Late Diagnosis, Unmasking, and
Finding Harmony Between Autism and ADHD

Foley Nannie Stone

ISBN: 978-1-7643271-0-7

This is a memoir based on my personal experiences and memories. While all events described are true to my recollection, some names and identifying details have been changed to protect privacy. Conversations have been reconstructed from memory and journals, representing the essence rather than verbatim transcripts.

This book describes my individual experience with autism and ADHD (AuDHD). Neurodivergence presents differently in every person, and my experiences should not be taken as representative of all autistic, ADHD, or AuDHD individuals.

The information in this book is not intended as medical advice or a substitute for professional diagnosis and treatment. If you suspect you may be neurodivergent, please consult with qualified healthcare professionals who specialize in adult autism and ADHD assessment.

The coping strategies and accommodations described are what worked for me personally. They may not work for everyone, and some may not be appropriate for your specific situation. Please use judgment and, when needed, professional guidance in implementing any strategies.

While I discuss mental health challenges including burnout, shutdown, and meltdown experiences, this book is not a replacement for mental health treatment. If you're experiencing mental health difficulties, please seek support from qualified professionals.

Views expressed about diagnosis, medication, therapy, and treatment approaches are my personal opinions based on my individual experience and should not be taken as professional recommendations.

Product recommendations are based on community feedback and personal experience. No affiliate relationships exist. Links and availability subject to change. This list is not exhaustive and represents resources available at time of publication. Your needs may vary - always consult with healthcare providers for medical advice.

Finally, language around neurodivergence evolves continuously. I've used identity-first language ("autistic person") as this is my preference and that of many in the autistic community, but I respect that others prefer person-first language. The terminology used reflects current understanding at the time of writing.

Table of Contents

Preface

This book began at 3 AM on a Tuesday, which feels fitting for an AuDHD brain that never quite understood the concept of "normal" timing. I was 27, recently diagnosed, and sitting on my bedroom floor surrounded by decades of evidence that everyone, including me had missed the obvious: I wasn't broken, lazy, or "too sensitive." I was autistic and ADHD, and had been my entire life.

The words poured out like water breaking through a dam, five years of unmasking, learning, failing, succeeding, and ultimately accepting that my brain operates on dual frequencies that sometimes harmonize and sometimes clash in spectacular chaos.

I wrote this book for the person I was before diagnosis, confused, exhausted, and convinced that everyone else had received an instruction manual for life that I'd somehow missed. I wrote it for the parents watching their children navigate a world that seems too loud, too bright, too much, and not enough all at once. I wrote it for the professionals who want to understand what AuDHD actually feels like from the inside.

But mostly, I wrote it because these stories need to exist. Not stories about "overcoming" neurodivergence, not tragedy narratives about suffering, but real, raw, complicated stories about what it's like to live with a brain that needs routine but craves novelty, seeks connection but requires solitude, processes everything and nothing simultaneously.

This is one story among millions. Your AuDHD might look nothing like mine. That's the point. We're not a monolith—we're a constellation of different experiences, each valid, each deserving of recognition and respect.

Foley Nannie Stone

Chapter 1: Wrong Frequency

The birthday party was supposed to be fun. That's what everyone kept saying, anyway.

Seven years old, and there I was, pressed against the kitchen wall while twenty kids ran screaming through my house. The streamers my mom had hung were this specific shade of metallic blue that made this weird rustling sound every time someone brushed past them. Nobody else seemed to notice. The cake sat on the counter – chocolate with vanilla frosting, exactly what I'd asked for – but the smell of it mixed with the pepperoni pizza made my stomach turn in ways I couldn't explain.

Here's the thing about being a kid with an undiagnosed AuDHD brain: you're constantly living in two different worlds at the same time. In one world, you're desperate to join the chaos, to be part of the group playing pin-the-tail-on-the-donkey. Your body practically vibrates with the need to move, to touch everything, to be in the middle of all that energy. But in the other world, you want everyone to leave immediately. The noise feels like sandpaper on your brain. The unpredictability of where people might run next makes your chest tight.

So you stand there, against the wall, watching your own birthday party happen around you like you're behind glass.

My mom found me there, of course. She always had this look – not quite worry, not quite frustration. More like she was trying to solve a puzzle she didn't have all the pieces for. "Sweetie, don't you want to play with your friends?"

Friends. Right. These kids from school who I sat near but never quite connected with. I knew their names, their favorite colors, what they brought for lunch. I could tell you that Sarah always wore her hair in two braids on Tuesdays and that Marcus tapped his pencil exactly four times before writing his name on his paper. But knowing these things and knowing how to be their friend? Completely different skills, turns out.

"I'm just taking a break," I told her, which became my go-to phrase for the next twenty years.

The Push and Pull Begins

Looking back now, I can see how that birthday party was just one example of the constant negotiation happening in my brain. Every single day was this exhausting dance between opposing needs.

Take bedtime, for instance. I needed my stuffed animals arranged in exactly the right order – bear, rabbit, elephant, always facing the door. The blanket had to be tucked in just so, not too tight but with no gaps where air could sneak in. My nightlight had to be the one with the soft yellow glow, not the harsh white one from the hallway. This routine was non-negotiable. It was the only way my brain would accept that yes, now it's time to sleep.

But then? Then my ADHD brain would kick in. *What if tomorrow we go to the park? What if I see a dog? What would happen if dogs could talk? Would they have accents? Do British dogs bark differently than American dogs?*

Two hours later, I'd still be wide awake, mentally organizing all the dogs in the world by theoretical accent, while simultaneously panicking because the routine hadn't worked and now everything felt wrong.

My parents tried everything. Warm milk (disgusting). Counting sheep (boring, plus why sheep?). Reading before bed (great, now I'm emotionally invested in what happens to the rabbit family and definitely can't sleep). They never got angry, just increasingly creative and progressively more tired-looking.

"Your brain is just very busy," my dad would say, rubbing his eyes. He meant it kindly, but even at seven, I heard what he wasn't saying: *Your brain is too busy. Your brain is wrong.*

The Daily Battlefield

School presented its own special kind of chaos. The structure should have been perfect for me – schedules, rules, clear expectations. And parts of it were. I loved knowing that math came after reading, that lunch was always at 11:30, that Friday meant library day. These anchors kept me from floating away entirely.

But the ADHD part of my brain treated structure like a challenge. *Sure, we're supposed to be doing worksheets, but have you noticed that the ceiling tile above Mrs. Peterson's desk has a water stain that looks exactly like a dragon? And if it's a dragon, does that mean dragons existed and left marks on ceiling tiles as proof? Should I tell someone about this discovery?*

Meanwhile, the autism part was frantically trying to follow every rule to the letter. Pencils must be sharpened but not too sharp. Raise your hand but not too often. Share with others but protect your special erasers that smell like fruit.

The contradiction was constant. Be social but not too loud. Pay attention but don't stare. Follow the rules but be creative. It was like being given a radio that could only tune into two stations at once, both playing different songs at full volume.

I started developing these little tricks to manage it all. I'd count ceiling tiles during story time to keep my body still while my brain raced. I'd organize my crayons by color gradient while listening to instructions, the repetitive sorting somehow making the words stick better. I'd volunteer to hand out papers because moving around the classroom made sitting still afterward slightly more bearable.

Nobody told me these were coping mechanisms. I just thought everyone had their own weird little systems for getting through the day.

Family Dynamics and Misunderstandings

My family didn't know what to do with me. Not in a mean way – they loved me fiercely. But I was like a puzzle where half the pieces were from one box and half from another, and they were trying to make a coherent picture without knowing two different images were involved.

My older sister was everything I wasn't. She could walk into a room full of strangers and make three friends before I'd figured out where to stand. She did her homework without being reminded, kept her room reasonably clean, and never had meltdowns about the seams in her socks.

"Why can't you just try to be more like your sister?" my mom asked once, after I'd spent forty-five minutes having a complete breakdown because my favorite shirt was in the wash and no other shirt felt right against my skin.

She apologized immediately. I could see she regretted it the second the words left her mouth. But the damage was done. The message was clear: whatever I was, it was wrong. I needed to try harder to be normal. To be easier.

The thing is, I was trying. Every single day, I was trying so hard it felt like my brain might explode from the effort. I tried to ignore the way fluorescent lights hummed at a frequency that made my teeth hurt. I tried to pretend I didn't notice that my teacher wore the same five outfits in the exact same rotation every week. I tried to act like I cared about the games other kids played at recess instead of spending that time organizing pebbles by size and color.

But trying to be normal when your brain is wired differently isn't like trying to learn math or trying to ride a bike. It's like trying to breathe underwater. You can hold your breath for a while, but eventually, you're going to need air.

The Beginning of Different

The word "different" started showing up a lot around third grade. Parent-teacher conferences became these events my parents would return from with tight smiles and folders full of papers about "learning styles" and "attention strategies."

"Your teacher says you're very creative," my mom would report, which even at eight I recognized as code for "your teacher doesn't know what to do with you."

Different. Special. Unique. Quirky. All these words that adults used when they meant "not quite right but we're too polite to say it."

I started watching other kids more carefully, like an anthropologist studying an unfamiliar culture. How did they know when it was okay to be silly and when they needed to be serious? How did they switch from one activity to another without feeling like their whole world was collapsing? How did they wear jeans without wanting to crawl out of their skin?

The more I watched, the more I realized I was operating on a completely different frequency than everyone else. It wasn't just that I was bad at being normal – it was like normal was a language I'd never been taught, in a frequency my brain couldn't quite tune into.

But here's what nobody tells you when you're eight and confused and trying so hard it hurts: different doesn't mean broken. Your brain isn't wrong, it's just running different software. Software that nobody's given you the manual for yet.

Some days I could almost catch the right frequency. I'd have a good day where everything clicked, where I remembered to raise my hand

and my socks didn't bother me and I could play with other kids without wanting to run away. Those days gave everyone hope. "See?" the adults would say. "You can do it when you try!"

But those days were exhausting in ways nobody could see. It was like holding a difficult pose – you can do it for a while, but eventually, your muscles start shaking and you have to let go. And when I let go, when I couldn't hold the pose anymore, everyone seemed surprised. Disappointed, even.

The birthday party ended, eventually. Kids went home with their goodie bags. My mom cleaned up while my dad did the dishes. My sister helped me open presents I was too overwhelmed to care about. And I sat in my room afterward, lining up my new toys in order of size, trying to make sense of a day that was supposed to be happy but felt like trying to watch two TV channels at once.

That night, as I arranged my stuffed animals in their exact right positions, I made a decision without really knowing I was making it. If I couldn't figure out how to be normal, I'd just have to get better at pretending. I'd learn to look like everyone else, even if I felt like I was broadcasting on a completely different frequency.

What I didn't know then – what would take me decades to understand – was that millions of other people were out there, trying to tune into the same impossible frequency, thinking they were the only ones who couldn't get the signal quite right.

Chapter 2: Volume Wars

Fourth grade was the year everything got louder. Not literally – though the cafeteria did seem to echo more, and Kyle Morrison had discovered he could make this piercing whistle that felt like someone was drilling directly into my skull. No, everything got louder in the sense that all the conflicts in my brain seemed to turn up their volume controls at the same time.

School had always been this weird mix of comfort and torture, but now the stakes felt higher. We weren't just learning addition anymore; we were doing long division with remainders. We weren't just reading picture books; we were writing book reports with topic sentences and supporting details. The rules were multiplying faster than I could learn them.

Here's what my brain did with structure: it clung to it desperately while simultaneously trying to escape it.

Every morning, I needed my routine. Wake up at exactly 6:45. Eat cereal (Cheerios, never Frosted Flakes – too sweet, too much change in texture as they got soggy). Brush teeth for exactly two minutes. Pack backpack in the same order: homework folder, reading book, lunch, pencil case on top. Any deviation from this routine felt like someone had rearranged all the furniture in my brain.

But then I'd get to school, where structure was everywhere, and my ADHD brain would revolt. *Why do we have to do math first? What if I want to think about dinosaurs right now? Did you know that T-Rex arms were actually super strong, just small? Wait, why is everyone taking out their math books?*

The Predictability Paradox

Mrs. Rodriguez had this whole system. Everything in her classroom had a place, a purpose, a rule. She wrote the schedule on the board every morning in the same purple marker. Math: 8:30-9:15. Reading: 9:15-10:00. She even had this timer that played a little song when we needed to transition between subjects.

This should have been perfect for me. And part of me – the autism part – absolutely loved it. I knew what was coming. I could prepare myself. When the timer played its little tune, I could start the mental process of putting away one subject and taking out another.

But the ADHD part of my brain treated that timer like a starting gun at a race I didn't want to run. *Quick! Think of everything except what we're supposed to be doing! Remember that documentary about octopi? They have three hearts! Why three? Is one a backup? What happens if–*

"Eyes up here, please," Mrs. Rodriguez would say, and I'd realize I'd been staring at my pencil for five minutes, mentally designing an octopus-powered submarine.

The worst part was Silent Reading Time. Twenty minutes of sitting still, quietly, with a book. The autism part of my brain loved the clear expectations: be quiet, read your book, stay in your seat. Simple. Clean. Followable.

The ADHD part treated it like a form of torture specifically designed to make me combust. My legs would start bouncing. My fingers would tap. I'd read the same sentence seventeen times because my brain kept wondering if the author had pets and what they named them and whether fish count as pets if they don't know you exist.

I developed this system where I'd read one page, then allow myself thirty seconds to mentally redesign the classroom (the reading corner should definitely be by the window, not the door). Then another page. Then thirty seconds to count all the rectangular things I could see without moving my head. It was exhausting, but it was the only way I could get through without exploding.

9

Sensory Overload Meets Hyperactivity

Picture this: you're hypersensitive to every sound, smell, touch, and light in your environment. The fluorescent bulb above your desk buzzes at exactly the wrong frequency. Your shirt tag scratches your neck every time you move. The kid next to you smells like bubble gum and wet dog, and you can't figure out why.

Now add to that a body that desperately needs to move, to fidget, to explore, to touch everything. Your legs want to run. Your hands want to grab. Your whole being vibrates with unused energy.

That was every single school day for me.

I'd sit there, trying to focus on the math worksheet, but my brain was processing seventeen different inputs at once. The clock ticking (too loud). The smell of markers from art class (why did they make my head feel fuzzy?). The way the sunlight hit Jessica's hair and made it look like copper wire. The uncomfortable pressure of the chair against my back. The need to move, move, MOVE.

Sometimes it would all become too much, and I'd just... shut down. Not a dramatic meltdown – I saved those for home, where it was safer. But this quiet implosion where suddenly I couldn't process anything. Mrs. Rodriguez would ask me a question, and even though I knew the answer, the words would get stuck somewhere between my brain and my mouth.

"Use your words," she'd encourage, not unkindly.

But my words were trapped behind a wall of sensory static and hyperactive impulses. I'd sit there, knowing the answer, wanting to answer, completely unable to make my mouth work.

Other times, I'd overflow in the opposite direction. My hand would shoot up for every question, even ones I didn't know the answer to. I'd blurt out observations that had nothing to do with the lesson. I'd wiggle so much my chair would actually travel across the floor.

"Do you need to take a walk?" Mrs. Rodriguez would ask.

Yes. No. Both. Neither. I needed to run laps around the building AND sit perfectly still in absolute silence. I needed complete predictability AND constant novelty. I needed everyone to leave me alone AND someone to understand exactly what was happening in my brain.

Contradictory Feedback

Parent-teacher conference season was like waiting for a verdict in a trial where I didn't understand the charges.

"So talented," teachers would say. "Really bright. Creative. Interesting perspective."

My parents would start to relax.

"But," the teacher would continue, and my parents' shoulders would tense again. "Needs to apply themselves more consistently. Has trouble with transitions. Sometimes seems like they're not paying attention, but then scores perfectly on tests. Very rigid about certain things but completely scattered about others."

The feedback was always contradictory:

- Too focused on details but misses the big picture
- Reads above grade level but can't summarize what they just read
- Exceptional memory for facts but forgets to turn in homework
- Needs to participate more but also needs to stop interrupting
- Should work more independently but also needs to ask for help

My parents would come home with these reports, trying to make sense of a child who was simultaneously gifted and struggling, ahead and behind, too much and not enough.

"Maybe we need to try harder," my mom would say, not to me but to my dad, like I wasn't sitting right there.

Try harder at what, exactly? I was already trying so hard that I'd fall asleep the second I got home from school, my brain completely depleted from managing all its contradictions.

The real kicker was standardized testing. I'd ace the actual test – hyperfocus was perfect for those bubble sheets – but the preparation would nearly break me. The practice tests, the changes in routine, the pressure to sit still for extended periods. The autism part needed to follow every instruction perfectly. The ADHD part wanted to create patterns in the bubble sheet that looked like pictures.

"You're so smart," teachers would say, looking at my test scores. "If you just applied yourself more consistently..."

But consistency required a different kind of brain than the one I had. My brain was more like a radio that kept switching between AM and FM without warning. Sometimes you'd get classical music, sometimes heavy metal, sometimes just static. I couldn't control the dial.

The Battle Nobody Saw

The volume wars weren't just about actual volume – though seriously, why did everything have to be so loud? They were about the constant battle between opposing needs, playing out invisibly inside my head every single day.

Getting dressed in the morning could take forty-five minutes. Not because I was being difficult, but because I needed clothes that met both my sensory needs (soft, no tags, right pressure) and my ADHD need for stimulation (interesting colors, patterns that gave my eyes something to do). My mom would find me sitting on my floor, surrounded by rejected outfits, crying because nothing felt right.

"Just pick something," she'd say, frustration creeping into her voice.

But I couldn't just pick something. The wrong clothes meant a whole day of my skin feeling like it was staging a revolt. It meant not being able to concentrate on anything except how wrong everything felt.

Homework was another battlefield. I needed absolute silence to focus (autism), but silence made my ADHD brain create its own noise. I needed background music, but only instrumental, and only if it didn't have any surprising tempo changes. I needed to sit at my desk, in exactly the right position, with exactly the right pencil. But I also needed to stand, to pace, to do handstands between math problems.

My dad built me this whole "homework station" with everything perfectly organized. It lasted about a week before my ADHD brain decided it was boring and started doing homework under the dining room table instead.

The worst part? I couldn't explain any of this. I didn't have words for the war happening in my brain. All I knew was that everything felt too hard, too much, too contradictory. I was exhausting myself trying to be what everyone needed me to be, and I was failing at all of it.

Finding My Volume

Somewhere around the middle of fourth grade, I started to figure out tiny ways to moderate my own volume. Not fix it – nothing was broken, even though I didn't know that yet. Just... adjust the dial a little.

I discovered that if I read while walking on the treadmill my dad had in the basement, I could actually finish a chapter without my brain escaping. The movement satisfied the ADHD need while the predictable rhythm soothed the autism need for pattern.

I learned that I could survive Loud Classroom Things if I pressed my palms against my ears just enough to muffle the sound but not enough for anyone to notice. It looked like I was thinking really hard, when actually I was just trying not to scream from the chaos.

I started carrying tiny objects in my pockets – a smooth stone, a piece of velvet, a rubber band. When the volume got too loud, I could touch these things secretly, giving my brain something predictable and controllable to focus on.

These weren't solutions. They were survival tactics. But they were mine, developed through trial and error, through countless days of being too much and not enough at the same time.

Mrs. Rodriguez noticed, I think. She started letting me deliver things to the office when I got extra wiggly. She moved my seat to the corner where I could see everything without everyone seeing me. She stopped calling on me when I was clearly somewhere else in my head, waiting until I came back on my own.

Small mercies that felt huge at the time.

The volume wars didn't end in fourth grade. If anything, they were just warming up for the chaos of middle school. But that year taught me something important: my brain was playing two different songs at once, and maybe that was okay. Maybe the point wasn't to turn one off but to find a way to make them harmonize.

Some days, I could almost hear it – this moment where the structure-needing autism brain and the novelty-seeking ADHD brain would sync up, creating something that wasn't normal but was uniquely mine. Those moments were rare, but they existed.

And even though I didn't have words for it yet, even though I wouldn't understand for years what was actually happening, I started to realize that maybe the problem wasn't my volume at all.

Maybe everyone else just needed better ears.

Chapter 3: Crossed Signals

Middle school hit like a freight train carrying a cargo of pure social confusion.

Suddenly, the rules I'd spent years trying to decode? They all changed. Everything that had been wrong in elementary school was still wrong, but now there were seventeen new ways to be wrong that nobody had warned me about. Wearing the wrong brand of sneakers. Laughing at the wrong moment. Standing too close or too far away. Using words that were apparently childish now, even though they were perfectly good words last year.

The first day of seventh grade, I walked into school with my perfectly organized binder system – color-coded by subject, tabs labeled in my neatest handwriting. I'd spent three hours setting it up, finding deep satisfaction in the order of it all. This was going to be the year I got it right.

By lunch, I'd learned that caring about your binder was social suicide.

"Why do you try so hard?" this girl asked me, not meanly, just genuinely puzzled. Like I was a math problem that didn't quite compute.

Because if I don't try this hard at organization, my ADHD brain will scatter my homework across three dimensions and possibly into alternate universes, I wanted to say. Instead, I shrugged and started carrying my papers crumpled in my backpack like everyone else, dying a little inside each time I saw a wrinkled worksheet.

The Exhausting Art of Connection

Here's something nobody talks about: wanting friends and being able to maintain friendships are two completely different skill sets.

I wanted friends desperately. I'd watch groups of kids laughing together and feel this ache in my chest, this bone-deep loneliness that felt like being hungry for something I couldn't name. The human connection part of my brain craved belonging, understanding, those inside jokes everyone else seemed to have.

But the actual mechanics of friendship? Absolutely mystifying.

There was this girl, Emma, who sat next to me in English. She liked the same books I did, and we'd have these amazing conversations about character motivations and plot holes. For twenty minutes, I'd feel normal. Connected. Like maybe I'd finally figured out this whole friendship thing.

Then she'd want to continue the conversation after class, walking through the hallway, and everything would fall apart. Walking and talking at the same time meant navigating crowds (sensory nightmare), maintaining conversation (executive function overload), and somehow not running into walls (spatial awareness? what's that?). By the time we got to her locker, I'd be so overwhelmed that I'd just... shut down. Stand there awkwardly while she waited for me to respond to something I hadn't even heard.

After a few weeks, she stopped waiting for me after class.

The ADHD part of my brain approached friendship like a puppy – *NEW PERSON! TELL THEM EVERYTHING! SHARE ALL THE THOUGHTS! BE BEST FRIENDS IMMEDIATELY!* I'd meet someone who seemed interesting and mentally plan our entire future friendship, complete with inside jokes we didn't have yet.

But the autism part needed friendship to follow rules, patterns, predictable rhythms. When someone didn't text back in the same timeframe they usually did, I'd spiral. Did I say something wrong?

Were they mad? Were we still friends? The uncertainty was unbearable.

Early Masking Strategies

Somewhere around eighth grade, I became a social scientist studying my own species.

I started keeping mental notes about how normal people acted. Jenny always tilted her head when she listened – people seemed to like that. Marcus made this specific laugh when something wasn't actually funny but social convention required laughing – I practiced it in the mirror until I could reproduce it perfectly. There was this specific way people said "hey" in the hallway – not too enthusiastic, not too flat, just this casual acknowledgment of existence.

I developed what I now know was a mask, though at the time I just thought of it as my "school self." School Self laughed at the right moments (usually about half a second after everyone else, once I'd confirmed it was appropriate). School Self knew which topics were acceptable (TV shows, complaints about homework, weekend plans) and which would mark you as weird (detailed explanations of your current hyperfixation, unusual facts about serial killers, why the cafeteria's fluorescent lights were clearly designed by someone who hated children).

School Self was exhausting to maintain.

By the time I got home each day, I was completely depleted. My mom would ask about my day, and I'd have nothing left. I'd grunt something noncommittal and disappear into my room, where I could finally stop performing.

In my room, I could organize my rock collection by geological classification. I could read the same book for the fifteenth time, finding comfort in knowing exactly what would happen next. I could sit in my closet with the door closed, in the dark, in the quiet, and just... exist without performing existence for anyone else.

17

"You're like a different person at home," my mom observed once, watching me have a complete meltdown over my sister borrowing my calculator without asking.

She was right. At home, I didn't have the energy to maintain the mask. At home, all the suppressed sensory overwhelm and social exhaustion and executive dysfunction came pouring out. Every minor frustration became a major catastrophe. Every unexpected change was a betrayal by the universe itself.

My family got the worst of me because they got the real me – the one too tired to pretend everything was fine.

Special Interests: The Rotating Obsessions

Then there were the special interests. Oh man, the special interests.

The autism part of my brain would latch onto something with the intensity of a thousand suns. When I discovered astronomy in seventh grade, I didn't just like space – I breathed it. I memorized the distance from Earth to every planet. I knew the composition of Jupiter's atmosphere and could list all of Saturn's moons in order of discovery. I'd stay up until 3 AM reading about black holes, vibrating with excitement about event horizons and spacetime distortion.

For three months, I was going to be an astrophysicist. No question. This was my calling, my destiny, the thing that finally made sense in my chaotic brain.

Then, just as suddenly, the ADHD part would get bored. The intense fascination would evaporate overnight, leaving me confused and somehow bereft. All those hours learning about space, and now my brain just... didn't care anymore?

Next came marine biology. Then forensic science. Then World War II history. Then etymology. Each obsession followed the same pattern: discover topic, consume everything about it with hyperfocus

18

intensity, talk about nothing else, drive everyone around me insane with facts they didn't ask for, then wake up one day with zero interest in it.

The worst part was the social fallout. I'd finally find someone who would tolerate my endless monologues about my current obsession, only to abandon the topic entirely just as they were getting interested. People started avoiding me, not because they disliked me, but because they never knew which version of me they were going to get.

"Remember when you were obsessed with sharks?" someone would say, trying to connect.

But shark-obsessed me might as well have been a different person. Current me was all about ancient Rome, and I couldn't access that shark enthusiasm anymore no matter how hard I tried.

The Push-Pull of Teen Identity

Being a teenager is hard for everyone, but being a teenager with an undiagnosed AuDHD brain was like trying to solve an equation where the variables kept changing.

Everyone was figuring out who they were, but I couldn't even maintain a consistent self from day to day. Monday me might be quiet and studious, hyperfocused on getting perfect grades. Tuesday me couldn't sit still, brain racing with ideas for a novel I'd never write. Wednesday me would have a sensory overload in the cafeteria and spend lunch hiding in the bathroom. Thursday me would impulsively sign up for drama club, convinced I'd finally found my people. Friday me would skip drama club because the thought of improvisation made me want to throw up.

The autism part wanted to find my group, my identity, my place in the social ecosystem. But it needed that identity to be stable, predictable, safe. The ADHD part wanted to try everything, be everything, experience everything. It was exhausted by routine and energized by novelty.

Other kids seemed to pick a lane. The athletes. The theater kids. The smart kids. The rebels. They had groups, styles, predictable patterns of behavior. But I couldn't pick a lane because I needed all the lanes and none of them at the same time.

I tried on identities like clothes, none of them fitting quite right. For a week, I'd be the artistic one, carrying sketchbooks and wearing all black. Then I'd be the academic one, joining debate team and living in the library. Then the class clown, making inappropriate jokes at inappropriate times and immediately regretting it.

Each identity felt real in the moment. When I was obsessed with guitar, I genuinely believed I'd become a musician. When I discovered photography, I knew with absolute certainty that this was my calling. But then the interest would fade, leaving me with an expensive guitar I couldn't bear to touch and a camera that made me feel guilty every time I saw it.

"You just haven't found yourself yet," my dad would say, trying to be supportive.

But how do you find yourself when yourself keeps changing? How do you know who you are when your brain can't even agree with itself about what it wants for lunch?

The Social Mine Field

Social interactions in middle school were like navigating a minefield while wearing a blindfold and noise-canceling headphones.

There were all these unwritten rules that everyone else seemed to download automatically. Don't stand too close to someone at their locker. Don't be the first one to finish your test. Don't care too much about anything academic. Don't admit you still watch cartoons. Don't, don't, don't.

But also: Do laugh at the right jokes. Do know the right music. Do have opinions about things that don't matter. Do pretend you understand references you don't. Do, do, do.

Group projects were special torture. The autism part needed clear roles and responsibilities, detailed planning, and everyone following through on their commitments. The ADHD part would volunteer for everything, then forget to do half of it, then pull an all-nighter trying to save the project while having a panic attack about letting everyone down.

I remember this one science project about ecosystems. I'd volunteered to make the visual presentation because hyperfocus and art supplies seemed like a good combination. I spent twelve straight hours creating this elaborate diorama with tiny handmade animals and perfectly scaled trees. It was beautiful. It was also completely wrong because I'd hyperfocused on the creation and forgotten to actually research the ecosystem we were assigned.

My group members looked at my elaborate rainforest diorama – we were supposed to do the tundra – with expressions I'll never forget. Not angry, just... baffled. Like I was an alien who'd tried to complete human homework but misunderstood the fundamental concept.

"It's really... detailed," one of them said finally.

I wanted to disappear into the floor. All that work, all that focus, and I'd failed at the most basic requirement: paying attention to the actual assignment.

The Weight of Not Knowing

The hardest part about being an undiagnosed AuDHD teenager wasn't any single symptom or struggle. It was the not knowing. The constant, exhausting confusion about why everything felt so much harder for me than everyone else.

I watched my classmates navigate social situations, academic challenges, and identity formation with what looked like ease. Sure, everyone struggled sometimes, but they didn't seem to be fighting their own brains every step of the way.

"You're just overthinking things," people would say when I tried to explain how hard it was to know when someone was joking versus serious.

"Everyone feels awkward sometimes," they'd reassure me when I described the sensory hell of school dances.

"You just need to apply yourself," teachers would say when my grades swung wildly between A's and F's with no middle ground.

But it wasn't just overthinking or normal awkwardness or lack of application. It was something deeper, more fundamental. Something I had no words for.

So I started believing what everyone implied: that I was just bad at being a person. That everyone else found it this hard but was better at handling it. That my struggles were character flaws, personal failures, evidence of weakness.

I developed anxiety about my anxiety. Depression about my depression. Shame about my shame. Layer upon layer of self-doubt and self-blame, all because nobody recognized the war happening in my brain.

By the end of middle school, I was exhausted. Not physically tired – though that too – but soul-deep exhausted from trying to be normal, failing, and not understanding why. The masks I wore were getting heavier. The gap between who I was and who I needed to be was getting wider.

But somehow, through all of it, there were moments. Brief flashes where everything aligned. Where my hyperfocus and special interest would combine into something brilliant. Where my different perspective would solve a problem nobody else could see. Where my intensity and passion would connect with someone else's, and for a minute, I didn't feel like an alien.

Those moments kept me going. They were crossed signals that occasionally, miraculously, lined up just right. They whispered that maybe, possibly, there wasn't something wrong with me.

Maybe I was just tuned to a frequency that hadn't been discovered yet.

Chapter 4: Feedback Loop

College was supposed to be different. That's what everyone said, anyway. "You'll find your people in college." "College is where you can finally be yourself." "Everything changes in college."

They were right, but not in the ways they meant.

What actually changed was that now I was responsible for managing all my contradictions without any external structure. No parents making sure I ate regular meals. No forced routine of getting up and going to school. No teachers noticing if I didn't show up. Just me, my undiagnosed AuDHD brain, and an overwhelming amount of freedom that felt more like free fall.

The first week was intoxicating. I could arrange my dorm room exactly how I wanted it. I could create my own schedule. I could eat the same safe food for every meal without anyone commenting. I could stay up until 4 AM researching whatever caught my interest without anyone telling me to go to bed.

By week two, I realized I'd created my own perfect storm.

The Illusion of Normal

I chose my college carefully – small enough not to be overwhelming, large enough to disappear when needed. I picked a major that seemed to match my current hyperfocus (psychology, ironically). I even joined clubs during orientation week, determined that this time would be different.

For about a month, I maintained the illusion beautifully. I showed up to classes with color-coded notebooks. I attended club meetings. I made friendly conversation with my roommate. I even went to a few parties, standing in corners nursing the same red cup all night, masking so hard my face hurt from fake smiling.

Look at me, being normal. Finally figuring it out. Finally getting it right.

Then the executive dysfunction hit like it had been saving up energy for nineteen years.

I'd sit in my dorm room, fully aware that I had class in ten minutes, completely unable to make my body move. Not depressed, exactly. Not anxious, specifically. Just... stuck. Like someone had disconnected the wire between intention and action.

My autism brain would scream about the broken routine, the missed class, the disrupted schedule. My ADHD brain would immediately distract me with seventeen other things I could be doing instead. An hour later, I'd "come to" researching the history of Viking navigation techniques, having missed not just one class but two, with no memory of how I'd gotten from "I should go to class" to "but seriously, how did they use crystals to navigate?"

Code-Switching Olympics

If middle school social dynamics were a minefield, college was more like competing in the Olympics while juggling flaming torches.

There was Classroom Me, who needed to appear engaged but not too eager, smart but not show-offy. There was Dorm Me, who had to be friendly but not clingy with my roommate who clearly thought I was weird but was too polite to say so. There was Party Me, who had to seem relaxed in sensory hell, making appropriate small talk while music pounded so loud I could feel it in my teeth.

Then there was Work Me. I got a part-time job at the library, thinking the quiet environment would be perfect. And it was, for the autism part. The predictable tasks, the organizational systems, the blessed quiet. But the ADHD part was dying of boredom, and I'd find myself reorganizing sections that didn't need reorganizing just to have something to do.

Each version of me had different scripts, different energy levels, different tolerance thresholds. The constant switching was exhausting. Some days I'd lose track of which version I was supposed to be, and Real Me would leak through – info-dumping about my latest obsession to a confused classmate, or having a minor meltdown when the cafeteria changed their schedule without warning.

"You're so random," people would say, which I learned was code for "you're weird but I'm trying to be nice about it."

The Hyperfocus Achievement Trap

Here's something nobody warns you about: being really good at something when your brain decides to cooperate can be worse than being consistently mediocre.

When hyperfocus kicked in, I was unstoppable. I wrote a thirty-page paper on cognitive dissonance that my professor called "graduate-level work." I learned basic Mandarin in six weeks just because I got interested in Chinese poetry. I redesigned the entire filing system at the library, creating something so efficient my boss actually gave me a raise.

These bursts of brilliance set expectations I couldn't maintain. Professors would see that thirty-page paper and expect that level of work consistently. They'd be confused and disappointed when my next assignment was three pages of barely coherent rambling turned in two days late because executive dysfunction had held my brain hostage.

"I know you can do better," they'd say. "I've seen what you're capable of."

But what I was capable of on a hyperfocus day and what I was capable of on a regular day were completely different things. It was like they'd seen me run a marathon once and now expected me to do it every day, not understanding that I'd used up six months of running energy in that single race.

The ADHD part would procrastinate until the last possible second, then the autism part would have a meltdown about the broken routine and imperfect work. I'd turn in assignments that were either masterpieces or disasters, with nothing in between.

The Relationship Paradox

Then there was dating. Oh boy.

I met Alex in my abnormal psychology class (the irony wasn't lost on me). They laughed at my weird observations. They didn't seem to mind when I got excited about random topics. They even found my tendency to organize things "cute."

For three months, the relationship was my new hyperfocus. I memorized everything about them – their class schedule, their favorite coffee order, the exact way they liked their eggs. The autism part of my brain thrived on learning their patterns, predicting their needs. The ADHD part was intoxicated by the novelty, the excitement, the dopamine hit of new love.

But then the novelty wore off, as it always did. And suddenly, maintaining the relationship felt like another exhausting performance. I needed alone time to recharge, but also craved their attention. I wanted routine and predictability, but also got restless with too much sameness. I'd make plans enthusiastically, then dread them as they approached.

"I never know which version of you I'm going to get," Alex said during what would be our last fight. "Sometimes you're completely obsessed with me, and sometimes it's like I don't exist."

They weren't wrong. When they were in front of me, they were my entire world. When they weren't, I'd forget to text for days, not because I didn't care, but because object permanence and emotional consistency weren't things my brain did well.

The breakup was both devastating and a relief. Devastating because rejection always hit my rejection-sensitive dysphoria like a truck. Relief because I could stop performing the role of "good partner" that I never quite understood how to play.

The Growing Awareness

By junior year, the feedback loop was getting tighter and louder. Every failed attempt at normal, every confused look, every "you're so random" comment added to the mounting evidence that something was fundamentally different about me.

I started reading psychology textbooks beyond my assignments, searching for answers. ADHD seemed to fit some things – the executive dysfunction, the time blindness, the hyperactivity that I'd learned to internalize into anxiety. But it didn't explain the sensory issues, the need for routine, the social confusion that went deeper than just impulsivity.

Autism explained other pieces – the sensory overwhelm, the special interests, the difficulty with social cues. But everyone knew autism meant you couldn't make eye contact or have friends or function in society, right? I could do all those things. They were exhausting and I did them wrong half the time, but I could do them.

Neither diagnosis alone explained the push-pull, the constant internal contradiction, the feeling of being two different people trying to operate one body.

I started seeing the campus therapist, hoping for answers. She diagnosed me with anxiety and depression, which weren't wrong but felt like diagnosing someone with "bleeding" when they'd been stabbed. Sure, accurate, but missing the actual source of the problem.

"Have you considered that you might just be highly sensitive?" she suggested. "Maybe a bit of a perfectionist?"

I wanted to scream. I wasn't sensitive; I was overloaded. I wasn't perfectionist; I was desperate for something, anything, to work the way my brain expected it to.

First Jobs and Professional Disasters

Senior year meant internships and job applications and trying to imagine a future when I couldn't even imagine getting through the week.

I got an internship at a local nonprofit, drawn to the mission and the structured environment. The first month was great – new job honeymoon phase met hyperfocus, and I revolutionized their entire filing system. My supervisor was impressed. I was going to be amazing at this adult working thing.

Then the novelty wore off. The fluorescent lights started giving me headaches. The open office plan meant constant interruptions that shattered my focus. The unwritten social rules of office culture were even more complex than college. When was it appropriate to join a conversation? How did people know when meetings were really over versus when they were just transitioning to social chat?

I'd stay late trying to finish work I couldn't focus on during the day, then be too exhausted to function the next day, creating a spiral of declining performance. My supervisor, the same one who'd praised me a month earlier, started giving me concerned looks.

"You started so strong," she said in what was meant to be a helpful feedback session. "What changed?"

Everything. Nothing. My brain went from cooperation mode to rebellion mode, and I didn't know how to explain that without sounding like I was making excuses.

The Breaking Point Approaches

By the time graduation rolled around, I was running on empty. Four years of masking, code-switching, and forcing my brain into boxes it didn't fit had left me depleted in ways I couldn't articulate.

My parents were so proud. I'd graduated! With honors, even (thanks, hyperfocus). I had a degree, a job offer from another nonprofit that hadn't yet discovered how inconsistent I could be. I'd made it through college. I was a success story.

Except I wasn't. I was a barely functioning human held together by elaborate coping mechanisms, caffeine, and the constant fear that everyone was about to figure out I had no idea what I was doing.

The real world loomed, with its full-time jobs and office politics and the expectation that now, finally, I'd have my act together. No more excuses about being young or figuring things out. This was it. Real adult life.

The feedback loop was screaming now. Every strategy I'd developed was failing. Every mask was cracking. Every coping mechanism was becoming less effective. I was like a computer running too many programs, overheating, about to crash.

Something had to give.

But first, I had to survive my twenties, that special decade where you're expected to build a career, maintain relationships, manage a household, and somehow become a functional adult, all while your brain is playing tug-of-war with itself.

What could possibly go wrong?

Chapter 5: Performance Mode

The nonprofit job lasted exactly seven months.

Seven months of arriving at 8:29 AM every day because arriving at 8:30 felt late but 8:28 felt desperately early. Seven months of eating the same lunch at the same desk while pretending to be social in the break room. Seven months of my brain screaming in two different directions while my face smiled and said things like "Happy Monday!" and "Circle back on that later!"

The end came not with some dramatic meltdown but with a quiet dissolution. My supervisor called me into her office on a Tuesday. I knew it was coming – the autism part of my brain had been tracking the pattern of concerned looks and "check-ins" for weeks.

"This just isn't the right fit," she said, which was corporate speak for "You're too weird and inconsistent for us to deal with."

I nodded, smiled, thanked her for the opportunity. Made it all the way to my car before the mask cracked and I spent forty minutes in the parking lot, unable to cry because I was too overwhelmed to access the emotion, unable to leave because transition required executive function I didn't have.

The Mask Factory

After that, I became a professional mask manufacturer. Not literally – though honestly, that might have been easier. I mean I got really, really good at creating and maintaining elaborate personas for different situations.

There was Corporate Me, who wore blazers that made my skin crawl but looked "professional." Corporate Me arrived early, stayed late, and had practiced facial expressions for meetings: Interested

But Not Too Eager, Thoughtfully Considering, Collaborative Team Player. Corporate Me laughed at jokes about weekend plans I'd never have and contributed appropriate comments about TV shows I'd researched but never watched.

There was Social Me, who accepted invitations to happy hours I dreaded from the moment I said yes. Social Me could sustain exactly 47 minutes of appropriate conversation before the battery died. I knew this because I timed it. Multiple times. The consistency was actually kind of fascinating, in a horrible way.

There was Dating Me, version 2.0, updated after the Alex disaster. This version had learned to set expectations low, to warn people upfront that I was "quirky" and "needed a lot of alone time." Dating Me could perform intimacy for about three dates before the real me started leaking through the cracks.

Each mask required different energy levels, different scripts, different suppression strategies. Corporate Me couldn't stim, so I developed invisible stims – pressing my tongue against the roof of my mouth in patterns, clenching and unclenching my toes inside my shoes. Social Me couldn't info-dump, so I bit my tongue until it hurt when someone got a fact wrong. Dating Me couldn't have meltdowns about restaurant lighting, so I learned to quietly dissociate until the meal was over.

The thing about masks, though? They're not just exhausting to wear. They fundamentally change how you breathe.

Professional Camouflage

I got another job, this time at a marketing firm. The interview had gone well because interviews were performance art and I'd studied for this show. I knew to maintain eye contact for exactly three seconds before looking away (I counted: one Mississippi, two Mississippi, three Mississippi, glance at their forehead). I knew to mirror their body language with a two-second delay. I knew to ask questions that showed interest without seeming too intense.

33

"You really impressed us," the hiring manager said. "You seem like such a good fit for our culture."

Their culture, it turned out, was open office plans, constant collaboration, and "agile workflows" that changed every week. In other words, sensory and executive function hell designed by someone who'd never met a neurodivergent person.

But I was determined to make it work. I bought noise-canceling headphones and told everyone I focused better with music. I created elaborate systems to track the constantly changing priorities. I volunteered for tasks that let me work alone, then stayed until 10 PM to finish the collaborative work I couldn't focus on during the chaos of the day.

For six months, I was a model employee. My reviews were stellar. "Such attention to detail!" they said about my autism-driven need for perfection. "So creative!" they said about my ADHD tangents that accidentally produced innovative ideas. "Such dedication!" they said about my inability to leave tasks unfinished even if it meant working myself into the ground.

Nobody saw the full-body shutdown that happened the moment I got home. Nobody saw me eating cereal for dinner standing over the sink because cooking required executive function I'd used up by 10 AM. Nobody saw the weekends spent in bed, not depressed exactly, just completely depleted from five days of performing neurotypicality.

The Success Trap

Here's the thing about being good at masking: success makes it worse.

Every time I successfully performed normal, it reinforced everyone's expectation that I could keep doing it. Every "great job!" was another brick in the wall between who I was and who I had to pretend to be. Every promotion (yes, I got promoted – turns out obsessive attention to detail and working until you collapse looks like "leadership potential") meant more meetings, more social interaction, more performance.

I developed this reputation as someone who could handle anything. Difficult client? Give it to me – I'd hyperfocus on their needs until they were happy. Complex project? I'd either knock it out in a brilliant hyperfocus session or stay up for three days straight forcing my brain to cooperate. Team conflict? I'd studied human behavior so intensely trying to understand it that I could mediate better than people who actually understood emotions intuitively.

"You're so capable," my boss would say, piling more on my plate.

But capable was just code for "good at suffering quietly."

The autism part of my brain created increasingly elaborate systems to manage everything. Color-coded calendars. Detailed task lists. Backup plans for backup plans. The ADHD part would then forget the systems existed, create new ones, or hyperfocus on perfecting the system instead of doing the actual work.

I was promoted to team lead, which meant more money but also more meetings. Meetings were special torture. The fluorescent lights. The overlapping conversations. The social dynamics I had to track while also trying to follow the actual content. The expectation that I'd contribute ideas verbally, in real-time, without the processing time I needed.

I developed meeting strategies. I'd prepare scripts for likely topics. I'd volunteer to take notes so I'd have an excuse to look down instead of making eye contact. I'd schedule "urgent calls" immediately after so I could escape to the bathroom and decompress.

It worked. I looked successful. I looked normal. I looked like I had everything together.

I was also dying inside, one masked day at a time.

The Dating Show

Because apparently I enjoyed suffering, I also tried dating again. Multiple times. Each attempt following the same predictable pattern.

Matches on dating apps were easy – I could craft the perfect profile, send witty messages on my own schedule, present my best self in carefully curated doses. First dates were manageable – I had scripts, backup topics, and exit strategies.

But then came the hard part: sustaining it.

There was James, who thought my "quirks" were adorable until he realized they weren't quirks but fundamental aspects of how my brain worked. The third time I had to leave a restaurant because the music was too loud, he stopped finding it cute.

There was Maria, who loved how passionate I was about things until she realized I couldn't turn it off. Two-hour monologues about urban planning (my hyperfocus that month) weren't actually romantic, apparently.

There was Sam, who appreciated my "independence" until they realized it wasn't independence but an inability to maintain consistent emotional connection when they weren't physically present.

Each relationship followed the same arc: initial fascination (new person! dopamine!), intense bonding (hyperfocus on learning everything about them), gradual overwhelm (too much social demand), and eventual collapse (running out of masking energy).

"You're so hot and cold," Maria said during our breakup. "It's like you're two different people."

She wasn't wrong. I was at least two different people, possibly more, and none of them knew how to sustain a relationship while also maintaining basic functioning.

The Body Keeps Score

By age 25, my body started presenting the bill for all this masking.

Chronic migraines from the sensory overload I pushed through daily. IBS from the stress of constant performance. Insomnia from a brain that couldn't switch off. Random pain that doctors couldn't explain but I knew was from holding my body in unnatural positions to appear "normal."

"You're very tense," a massage therapist told me once, which was hilarious because I'd been holding tension in every muscle for so long I didn't know what relaxed felt like.

My doctor ran tests, found nothing wrong, and suggested stress management. I nodded, smiled, agreed to try yoga (lasted exactly one class – too many sensory inputs and social rules). Nobody connected the dots between my physical symptoms and the exhausting performance of being human.

I started calling in sick more often. Not lying, exactly – I was sick. Sick of pretending, sick of performing, sick of the enormous effort required to exist in a world built for brains that weren't constantly fighting themselves.

But sick days meant falling behind, which triggered the anxiety, which made the physical symptoms worse, which required more sick days. Another feedback loop, this one written in muscle tension and stomach acid.

The Cracks in the Foundation

The mask started slipping in small ways at first.

I'd forget to modulate my voice and suddenly be talking too loud or too fast. I'd miss social cues I usually caught, standing too close or laughing at the wrong moment. The scripts I'd memorized would get jumbled, and I'd respond to "How was your weekend?" with "Fine, thanks, and you?" even though they hadn't asked how I was.

Coworkers started noticing. "You okay?" became a constant refrain. "You seem... different."

Different from what? From the elaborate performance they'd been watching? From the mask I could no longer maintain perfectly? From the idea of me they'd constructed from my careful acting?

I started making mistakes at work. Not big ones at first – missed emails, forgotten attachments, showing up to the wrong meeting room. But for someone whose autism-driven perfectionism had been carrying the whole operation, any mistake felt catastrophic.

The ADHD brain would forget something, the autism brain would spiral about the broken pattern, and I'd end up paralyzed between the two, unable to move forward or let go.

My performance reviews started including words like "inconsistent" and "unfocused" and "needs improvement in communication." The same job I'd been excelling at was now apparently beyond my capabilities, not because the job had changed but because I couldn't maintain the mask anymore.

The Price of Passing

Here's what nobody tells you about successfully passing as neurotypical: the better you are at it, the less help you can ask for.

I couldn't explain to my boss that I needed accommodations because I'd spent three years proving I didn't. I couldn't tell my friends I was struggling because my whole relationship with them was based on being the one who had it together. I couldn't ask for understanding because I'd worked so hard to not need understanding.

The mask had become a prison of my own making.

I watched coworkers easily navigate situations that required all my energy. They'd chat before meetings, transition smoothly between tasks, handle unexpected changes without their entire world tilting. They weren't performing; they were just existing. The difference was so stark it physically hurt.

"You make everything look so easy," a new coworker said to me once, watching me juggle multiple projects.

I wanted to laugh. Or cry. Or explain that what looked easy was actually me running mental calculations constantly – how long to maintain eye contact, when to smile, what tone to use, how to sit, when to contribute, how to look engaged but not intense, how to be human in a way that didn't raise questions.

Instead, I smiled and said, "Thanks, just practice!"

Practice. Like I hadn't been practicing being a person for 25 years and still couldn't get it quite right.

The Beginning of the End

The moment I knew the performance was ending came on a random Wednesday. I was in a meeting, surrounded by people discussing marketing strategies, and I suddenly couldn't understand what anyone was saying. Not because of the words – I knew the words. But the meaning wouldn't connect. It was like they were speaking a language I'd memorized phonetically without understanding what any of it meant.

I excused myself, went to the bathroom, and sat in a stall for twenty minutes trying to remember how to be a person. My mask hadn't just slipped; it had shattered into pieces I didn't know how to reassemble.

That night, I went home and did something I'd never done before: I googled "autism ADHD adult diagnosis."

The first result was about something called AuDHD. Autism and ADHD, together, creating a unique neurological profile that was neither one nor the other but both simultaneously.

I read article after article, each one describing my life in ways I'd never been able to articulate. The push-pull. The contradictions. The exhausting performance of being human in a world built for different brains.

For the first time in 25 years, something made sense.

But making sense of it and knowing what to do about it were two very different things. I still had to show up to work tomorrow. I still had to perform. I still had to maintain the elaborate façade I'd built.

But now I knew it was a façade. Now I knew why everything was so hard.

And that knowledge, terrifying as it was, felt like the first real breath I'd taken in years.

Chapter 6: Echo Chamber

The worst part about masking isn't the exhaustion. It's not even the identity crisis of never knowing who you really are underneath all the performances. The worst part is that after a while, you can't hear your own voice anymore. Everything becomes an echo of what you think other people want to hear.

By 26, I was living in an echo chamber of my own making. Every response calibrated. Every reaction calculated. Every emotion filtered through the question: "Is this acceptable? Is this normal? Is this what they expect?"

My apartment was the only place the echoes stopped, and even there, they'd grown so loud I sometimes caught myself performing for an audience that didn't exist.

Relationships While Wearing a Mask

Sarah and I met at a friend's birthday party – the kind of sensory nightmare I only attended to maintain the illusion of being social. She was sitting outside on the porch, away from the noise, reading a book during a party. My brain did that thing where it hyperfocused on a person instead of a topic, and suddenly she was the most interesting human on the planet.

"Good book?" I asked, immediately cringing at the generic opening.

She looked up, smiled, and said, "I have no idea. I'm just hiding from the party."

For one unguarded moment, I laughed – really laughed, not the practiced social laugh – and said, "Oh thank god, me too."

That should have been my first clue that maybe, possibly, I could be real with her. But twenty-six years of masking habits don't break that easily.

Instead, I created Sarah Version of Me. She was like Regular Masking Me but carefully calibrated to what I thought Sarah wanted. Sarah liked quiet activities? Sarah Me was suddenly into museums and bookstores (I mean, I actually was, but now I performed being into them). Sarah was spontaneous? Sarah Me could totally handle last-minute plan changes (narrator: she could not).

For four months, I maintained the performance. I said yes to restaurants even when the lighting made me want to crawl under the table. I attended her friends' gatherings and performed Social Girlfriend so well that everyone loved me. I regulated my emotions, suppressed my stims, and modulated my enthusiasm to match what seemed appropriate.

"You're perfect," Sarah said one night, and my heart broke a little because she wasn't in love with me. She was in love with an elaborate performance of me.

The Loneliness of Never Being Known

Here's the thing about relationships when you're masking: you're always alone, even when you're with someone.

Sarah would tell me about her day, and I'd respond with appropriately timed "mmhmms" and questions, all while part of my brain was running constant calculations. *Is this enough eye contact? Too much? Should I touch her hand now? Is this the right facial expression for sympathy?*

When she stayed over, I couldn't do my bedtime routine. Couldn't arrange my stuffed animals (yes, at 26, shut up, they were comforting). Couldn't check the locks three times. Couldn't play the same song on repeat until my brain settled. So I'd lie there, rigid with the wrongness of it all, performing Relaxed Girlfriend Going to Sleep while my nervous system screamed.

She'd ask what was wrong, and I'd say "nothing," because how do you explain that everything is wrong when nothing has actually happened? How do you tell someone that their presence, which you want and chose, is also sensory torture? How do you say "I love you but being perceived is agony" without sounding absolutely unhinged?

You don't. You perform being fine until fine becomes another mask you can't take off.

The loneliest moment was when Sarah met my family. Watching her interact with them, I realized she had no idea who I really was. My family knew Pre-Mask Me, the one who had meltdowns about food textures and couldn't handle schedule changes. Sarah knew Mask Me, the one who was flexible and easygoing and definitely didn't eat the same safe foods for weeks at a time.

"You're so different around your family," she observed afterward.

"Yeah, families, right?" I deflected, but inside I was screaming because I wasn't different around my family. I was different around her. Around everyone. Different was my default state, and she'd never met the real me.

The Push-Pull in Intimate Spaces

The physical side of the relationship was its own special contradiction.

The ADHD part craved novelty, excitement, the dopamine hit of physical connection. The autism part needed very specific conditions – the right lighting, the right texture of sheets, the right amount of pressure. Not too much cologne. Not too little preparation time. Everything just so.

43

But explaining that makes you sound like a control freak or, worse, like you're not actually attracted to the person. So I performed that too. Pretended spontaneity was fine when it made my skin crawl. Pretended I liked surprise affection when unexpected touch sometimes felt like static shock. Pretended I was fully present when really I was calculating how long before I could reasonably need "space."

"You're so independent," Sarah would say, and it sounded like a compliment but felt like proof she didn't really see me. I wasn't independent; I was desperate for connection. I just needed that connection to happen in very specific ways that I couldn't explain without sounding broken.

The relationship ended not with a fight but with a fizzle. Sarah Me became too exhausting to maintain. I started pulling away, not because I didn't care but because I couldn't keep up the performance. She noticed, of course.

"It's like you've checked out," she said during what would be our last real conversation.

She was right. I had checked out. But I'd never really been checked in. How can you be present in a relationship when you're not even present in your own life?

Friendship as Performance Art

It wasn't just romantic relationships. Every friendship was a carefully orchestrated performance.

There was Work Friends Me, who grabbed drinks and complained about bosses and pretended to care about sports. There was College Friends Me, who still had energy for reunions and remembered inside jokes I'd documented in a spreadsheet to keep track of. There was Hobby Friends Me, who joined a book club during a hyperfocus phase and now had to pretend I still cared about reading the same way I had for those three intense months.

Each friend group knew a different version of me, and keeping the versions straight was exhausting. Work Friends Me was professional and put-together. College Friends Me was still young and fun. Book Club Me was intellectual and thoughtful.

The worst was when worlds collided. When a work friend wanted to hang out on weekends, or when college friends visited and wanted to see my "real life." I'd have to quick-change between masks, and sometimes I'd glitch – use the wrong voice, reference the wrong interest, forget which version of my history I'd shared with whom.

"You never mentioned you were into rock climbing," a work friend said once, seeing the gear in my apartment from a three-month hyperfixation I'd had two years ago.

"Oh, yeah, just dabbled," I said, shoving the very expensive equipment I'd obsessively researched and purchased into a closet, another monument to my brain's inability to maintain consistent interests.

The Energy Drain of Constant Monitoring

Every social interaction required constant internal monitoring.

Am I talking too much? Not enough? Is this interesting to them? My voice is getting too loud, bring it down. No, now it's too quiet. They looked at their phone – am I boring them? Quick, ask them a question. Wait, was that too personal? Why did I say that? Okay, they're laughing, was that a real laugh or a polite laugh? Check their body language. Are they angled toward me or away? Have I been making eye contact? Too much? Not enough? When did I last blink?

This ran in the background of every conversation, every hangout, every interaction. Even texting required analysis. Response time had to be calibrated – too fast seemed desperate, too slow seemed rude. Emoji usage had to match the other person's. Exclamation points carefully rationed.

45

By the time I got home from any social event, I was depleted in ways sleep couldn't fix. It wasn't just introversion – introverts recharge alone. This was more like... system failure from running too many programs at once.

Friends would text, "That was fun! Let's do it again soon!" and I'd stare at my phone, genuinely unable to determine if I'd had fun or just performed having fun so well that even I couldn't tell the difference anymore.

The Feedback Loop of False Intimacy

The echo chamber created this horrible feedback loop. The better I got at masking, the more people liked Mask Me. The more they liked Mask Me, the more trapped I became in the performance. The more trapped I became, the less possible it felt to ever show them Real Me.

"You're such a good listener," friends would say, not knowing that I'd learned to ask questions to avoid having to figure out appropriate personal sharing.

"You're so easy-going," they'd say, not seeing the white-knuckled grip I had on my anxiety as I pretended restaurant changes didn't make me want to scream.

"You never complain," they'd observe, not realizing I'd learned that my actual complaints – the lights are too bright, the tag in my shirt feels like sandpaper, I can hear the electricity in the walls – sounded crazy to neurotypical ears.

Each compliment was another bar in the cage. They loved who they thought I was, which meant they couldn't love who I actually was.

The Interior Monologue

Inside my head, the real me was screaming.

Constantly.

While Mask Me smiled and nodded and made appropriate small talk, Real Me was having a completely different experience.

This sweater is torture but it looks professional. The refrigerator in the break room is humming at a frequency that makes me want to cry. Janet is wearing a new perfume that smells like emotional violence. The meeting room is slightly colder than usual and now I can't concentrate on anything except the temperature. Someone moved my stapler half an inch and my entire desk feels wrong now.

But outside? Outside, I was Professional Employee, handling everything with grace and competence.

The disconnect between internal experience and external performance got so wide that sometimes I felt like I was watching myself from outside my body. There's Mask Me, saying the right things, doing the right things, being the right kind of person. And there's Real Me, floating somewhere above it all, wondering how long this could possibly continue.

When Worlds Collapse

The echo chamber started collapsing the day I had what I now know was autistic burnout but at the time just called "completely losing my shit."

It was a Tuesday. Someone had taken my parking spot. The coffee shop was out of my safe-food breakfast. My first meeting was moved to a different room with different lighting. Small things. Insignificant things. Things that Mask Me should have handled with ease.

Instead, I sat in my car in the parking garage and couldn't move. Not wouldn't – couldn't. My body wouldn't respond to my brain's commands. I sat there for three hours, fully conscious, completely unable to make myself get out of the car.

I called in sick, went home, and proceeded to have what can only be described as a complete system shutdown. I couldn't maintain any of the masks. Couldn't respond to texts. Couldn't pretend to care about things I was supposed to care about. Couldn't even pretend to be okay for the pizza delivery person.

Sarah called, concerned. Work called, concerned. Friends texted, concerned.

But I couldn't respond because I didn't know which version of me they were expecting to hear from.

The echo chamber had gotten so loud that when it suddenly went silent, I didn't know what my actual voice sounded like anymore. I'd been reflecting everyone else's expectations for so long that when the mirrors broke, there was nothing behind them but exhaustion and confusion and the dawning realization that I'd built an entire life that didn't actually fit me at all.

That night, lying in bed with my stuffed animals properly arranged for the first time in months, my weighted blanket at exactly the right pressure, my white noise machine at the perfect volume, I googled "autism ADHD adult women" for the hundredth time.

This time, I didn't just read. This time, I made an appointment for an evaluation.

Because the echo chamber was killing me, and I needed to find my actual voice before I forgot I'd ever had one at all.

Chapter 7: Interference Patterns

The burnout started slowly, then hit all at once. Like those videos of buildings being demolished – standing, standing, standing, gone.

For months, maybe years, I'd been running on borrowed energy. Taking from tomorrow to survive today. Operating at 150% capacity while my reserves quietly dwindled to nothing. I didn't notice the depletion because I was too busy maintaining the performance, keeping all the masks in place, managing the constant push-pull of my contradictory brain.

Then one morning, I woke up and couldn't remember how to be a person.

Not metaphorically. Literally couldn't remember the steps. Do I shower first or eat first? How many minutes do teeth-brushing take? What clothes do normal humans wear to offices? The scripts I'd memorized, the routines I'd forced myself into, the elaborate systems I'd built – all of it was just... gone.

I called in sick. Then called in sick again. Then again. Then stopped calling because even that required executive function I didn't have anymore.

When the Mask Doesn't Fit Anymore

The thing about autistic burnout that nobody tells you is that it's not like regular burnout where you're just tired and need a vacation. It's like your brain's operating system crashes and needs a complete reinstall, except you don't have the installation disc and wouldn't remember how to run it if you did.

Simple tasks became impossible. Making a sandwich required twenty-seven decisions I couldn't make. Going to the grocery store meant lights and sounds and people and choices – all things my brain could no longer process. I'd stand in my kitchen, knowing I was hungry, completely unable to bridge the gap between that knowledge and doing something about it.

My ADHD brain, usually so full of ideas and impulses, went quiet. Not peaceful quiet – empty quiet. Like a radio stuck between stations, playing static.

My autism brain, usually so desperate for routine and structure, couldn't remember what my routines were or why they mattered. I'd find myself sitting in the wrong chair, using the wrong mug, wearing the wrong socks, and feel vaguely disturbed without knowing why.

The masks I'd worn for so long wouldn't stay on anymore. I'd try to put on Professional Me to answer work emails, but the mask would slip off like it was made of water. I'd try to be Social Me to respond to concerned friends, but the words wouldn't come. All the versions of me I'd created were inaccessible, and underneath them was just... exhaustion.

The Shutdowns Nobody Sees

People think meltdowns are the violent ones – the screaming, crying, throwing things kind of breakdowns that make good TV drama. And yeah, I had those too, usually in the safety of my apartment where nobody could see.

But the shutdowns were worse.

A shutdown is like your brain putting itself in airplane mode without asking permission. Input stops processing. Output becomes impossible. You're conscious, aware, present, but completely unable to interact with the world.

I'd sit on my couch for hours, needing to use the bathroom but unable to make my body move. Not refusing to move – unable. The connection between intention and action severed. I'd watch the sun move across the wall, knowing time was passing, knowing there were things I should be doing, completely incapable of doing anything about it.

During one particularly bad shutdown, Sarah came by to check on me. She found me sitting exactly where she'd left me eight hours earlier, still wearing the same clothes, having not moved except to blink.

"What's wrong?" she kept asking. "Talk to me. Say something."

But I couldn't. My mouth wouldn't make words. My brain wouldn't form thoughts into sentences. I could hear her, understand her, feel her concern, but responding was like trying to speak underwater.

She ended up calling 911, convinced I was having some kind of stroke. The EMTs came, did tests, found nothing wrong. Because nothing was wrong, medically speaking. My brain had just decided it was done performing neurotypicality and shut down all non-essential functions.

"Conversion disorder," the ER doctor said, which is medical speak for "something's wrong but we don't know what."

They sent me home with a referral to a psychiatrist and a bill I couldn't afford.

The Physical Collapse

The burnout wasn't just mental. My body, after years of holding tension and suppressing stims and forcing itself into uncomfortable positions and clothes and situations, started breaking down too.

The migraines became daily. Light felt like knives. Sound felt like hammers. I started wearing sunglasses inside and earplugs to sleep, and even that wasn't enough.

My digestive system went completely haywire. Years of forcing myself to eat social foods, wrong-texture foods, wrong-temperature foods, foods that made my sensory system scream – it all caught up at once. I couldn't keep anything down except my few safe foods, and sometimes not even those.

The exhaustion was bone-deep. Not tired like you need sleep, but exhausted like your cells have forgotten how to make energy. I'd sleep for fourteen hours and wake up more tired than when I went to bed. Standing up required planning. Showering was a marathon. Existing was an Olympic sport I could no longer compete in.

My doctor ran every test imaginable. Thyroid, fine. Iron, fine. Vitamin levels, fine. Blood panels, all normal.

"Have you been under stress?" she asked, and I almost laughed because when had I not been under stress? My entire existence was stress. But that wasn't what she meant, so I just nodded and accepted the anxiety medication that wouldn't fix the problem because the problem wasn't anxiety. The problem was that I'd been running incompatible software for twenty-seven years and my system had finally crashed.

When Others Notice the Cracks

The worse I got, the more obvious it became that something was really wrong. Not just tired-wrong or stressed-wrong, but fundamentally, systematically wrong.

My boss called me into a meeting when I finally returned to work after two weeks of sick leave.

"We're concerned," she said, in that HR-trained voice that meant 'we're documenting this conversation.' "Your performance has been... inconsistent."

Inconsistent. Because sometimes I could hyperfocus and produce brilliant work, and other times I'd stare at my computer screen for hours, unable to remember what I was supposed to be doing. Because sometimes my mask would hold long enough for a meeting, and other times I'd have to excuse myself because the fluorescent lights were making me feel like my skin was trying to crawl off my body.

"Maybe you should consider whether this position is right for you," she suggested, which was corporate speak for "please quit so we don't have to fire you."

Friends started pulling away too. Not cruelly, just confused by the version of me that was emerging from the wreckage of burnout.

"You're different," they'd say. "You've changed."

But I hadn't changed. I'd just stopped being able to pretend. The me they were seeing now – the one who couldn't handle restaurant changes, who info-dumped about random topics, who sometimes went nonverbal mid-conversation – that had always been me. They'd just never seen it before because I'd been such a good actor.

Sarah tried to stick around, but how do you maintain a relationship with someone when you can't maintain basic functioning?

"I don't know how to help you," she said during what would be our last conversation. "I don't even know who you are anymore."

"Neither do I," I told her, and it was the most honest thing I'd said in our entire relationship.

The Confession Circuit

As the masks crumbled, truths started spilling out.

I told my mom about the eating issues – how I'd been cycling through the same five safe foods for months because everything else made me gag. She looked horrified, then guilty, remembering all those childhood dinners that ended in tears.

I told my sister about the stimming – how I'd been secretly rocking and flapping and pressing my hands together my entire life, just hidden where nobody could see. She said she'd noticed but thought I'd grown out of it.

I told my doctor about the sensory issues – really told her, not just mentioned them. About how clothing felt like punishment, how lights felt like assault, how the world was constantly too much. She looked at me like puzzle pieces were finally clicking together.

"Have you ever been evaluated for autism?" she asked.

"I'm not autistic," I said automatically. "I have friends. I had a girlfriend. I have a job."

She raised an eyebrow. "Had?"

Oh. Right.

"ADHD?" she suggested.

"I mean, maybe, but I'm not hyperactive," I said, while literally bouncing my leg so hard the exam table was shaking.

She gave me some referrals. I took them, put them in my bag, and didn't call for three more months because executive dysfunction is real and phone calls are terrifying.

The Relief of Giving Up

There's something almost peaceful about complete collapse. When you can't maintain any masks, when you can't meet any expectations, when you can't perform any version of normal, there's nothing left to lose.

I stopped trying to maintain friendships that required me to be someone I wasn't. Stopped responding to texts that required emotional energy I didn't have. Stopped pretending to care about things I didn't actually care about.

I quit my job – or rather, agreed to resign in exchange for two weeks of severance and no questions asked. Moved back in with my parents, which felt like failure but also like the first time I could breathe in years.

In my childhood bedroom, surrounded by things from before I learned to mask so thoroughly, I started stimming openly for the first time in decades. Rocking while I read. Flapping when I was excited. Humming the same sound over and over because it made my nervous system feel safe.

My parents didn't know what to do with this version of me. But at least it was a real version.

"We always knew you were different," my mom said one night, watching me arrange my food in patterns before eating. "We just didn't know how to help."

"I didn't know I needed help," I told her. "I thought everyone felt like this and was just better at handling it."

The Glitches in the Matrix

As I started to rebuild – slowly, carefully, without masks this time – I began noticing all the glitches I'd been ignoring.

How I could remember every word of a conversation from ten years ago but couldn't remember if I'd eaten lunch. How I needed absolute silence to focus but also needed background noise to think. How I craved deep pressure but couldn't stand light touch. How I desperately wanted routine but also desperately needed novelty.

These weren't bugs in my programming. They were features of a operating system I'd never had the manual for.

I started keeping notes, documenting the patterns. The autism brain needed structure, routine, predictability. The ADHD brain needed stimulation, novelty, flexibility. When they aligned – when I found something new that could become a routine, or when a special interest provided both structure and stimulation – I thrived. When they fought, I crashed.

The interference patterns weren't random. They were predictable, if you knew what to look for.

But knowing what to look for required knowing what you were looking at in the first place.

Which is how, at 27, burned out and broken down, living in my childhood bedroom and stimming freely for the first time in decades, I finally made the phone call to get evaluated.

Because maybe, possibly, if I knew what my brain actually was instead of what I'd been pretending it was, I could learn to work with it instead of against it.

Maybe the interference patterns could become harmonies.

Maybe.

But first, I had to stop trying to be neurotypical and start figuring out who I actually was.

Chapter 8: Breaking Point

The neuropsychologist's office was beige. Aggressively, overwhelmingly beige. Beige walls, beige carpet, beige chairs that made that specific squeak-crunch sound when you sat down. The kind of beige that someone probably thought was "calming" but actually felt like sensory static.

I'd rescheduled this appointment four times. Not because I didn't want answers – I desperately wanted answers – but because making phone calls required executive function I didn't have, and keeping appointments meant remembering they existed, and the whole process felt like trying to solve a Rubik's cube while wearing oven mitts.

But here I was, finally, at 27 years old, sitting in a beige chair while a woman with kind eyes and a clipboard asked me questions about my childhood.

"Tell me about school," she said.

Where do I even start? The hour-long meltdowns about homework? The color-coded systems that worked for exactly three days before my brain rejected them? The report cards that said "so much potential" in teacher-speak for "smart but weird"?

"It was... complicated," I said, which was like describing the ocean as "damp."

She smiled like she'd heard that before. "Take your time."

The Evaluation Marathon

The evaluation took three sessions, each four hours long. Twelve hours of tests, questions, puzzles, and tasks that made my brain feel like it was being turned inside out and examined under a microscope.

There were IQ tests where some parts felt laughably easy and others made me want to cry. Pattern recognition that my brain did instantly. Word problems that made perfect sense. Then verbal instructions I forgot before she finished speaking. Tasks requiring me to remember sequences that evaporated from my mind like water.

"I need you to repeat back these numbers in reverse order," she said.

My brain immediately started playing the Jeopardy theme song, because apparently, that was more important than remembering numbers.

There were questionnaires with questions like "Do you find social situations easy?" (What counts as easy? Easy compared to what? Which social situations? Does online count? What about parallel play? What if–)

"Just answer based on your first instinct," she said, noticing I'd been staring at question one for five minutes.

My first instinct was to research the validity of the questionnaire, the credentials of its creator, and the statistical reliability of self-reporting before answering, but I didn't think that's what she meant.

The Mirror of History

The worst part was the developmental history. My mom came to one session, armed with baby books and report cards and twenty-seven years of worried observations she'd never known what to do with.

"She lined up her toys obsessively," my mom told the neuropsychologist. "Everything had to be in rainbow order. If we moved one, she'd notice immediately and have a complete meltdown."

I wanted to argue that it wasn't obsessive, it was logical. Rainbow order made sense. It followed the light spectrum. Why would you organize colors any other way?

"But then she'd also lose things constantly," my mom continued. "She'd put something down and it would just... vanish from her awareness. We'd find homework completed perfectly and shoved under her bed. Permission slips in the refrigerator. Library books in the bathroom cabinet."

The neuropsychologist nodded, writing notes. "What about friendships?"

My mom sighed. "She'd make intense friendships, talk about someone constantly for weeks, then suddenly act like they didn't exist. Or she'd want friends but couldn't maintain the relationships. Kids would come over once and never want to come back."

"They were boring," I muttered. "They didn't want to organize rocks by geological classification or create elaborate ranking systems for different types of clouds."

"You ranked clouds?" the neuropsychologist asked, sounding genuinely interested.

"Cumulus clouds are obviously superior," I said automatically. "They have the best structure-to-aesthetic ratio. Cirrus are too wispy, stratus are too boring, but cumulus have that perfect cotton-ball quality that–" I stopped, realizing I was doing it again. The info-dumping thing that made people's eyes glaze over.

But she was still writing, still looking interested. "Continue," she said.

So I did. For twenty minutes. About clouds. And she just... let me.

The Crisis Gallery

"Tell me about your work history," she said during session two.

I laughed, but it wasn't funny. "Which failure would you like to hear about first?"

The job where I revolutionized their filing system then forgot to show up for a week because I got hyperfocused on learning origami? The one where I was promoted three times in six months then had a complete meltdown because they changed the coffee brand in the break room? The one where I was the best employee they'd ever had for exactly four months before burning out so completely I couldn't remember my own job title?

"All of it," she said. "The patterns are what matter."

So I told her about the cycle. The initial excitement and hyperfocus. The elaborate systems I'd create to manage everything. The praise and recognition when those systems worked. The gradual overwhelm as novelty wore off. The increasing sensory sensitivities. The mask getting heavier. The mistakes starting. The shame spiral. The shutdown. The inevitable collapse.

"Every job?" she asked.

"Every job. Every relationship. Every hobby. Every friendship. Everything."

She looked at her notes. "How long does the cycle usually last?"

"Three to six months for jobs. Two to four months for relationships. Hobbies can be anywhere from three days to three months. Friendships..." I tried to calculate. "Depends on how often I have to see them."

"And you've never found anything sustainable?"

"I thought I was just bad at being a person," I said. "Like everyone else had gotten an instruction manual for life and I was just improvising badly."

The Moment of Recognition

During the third session, she gave me a scenario: "You're at a party. You don't know many people. It's loud, crowded, and someone you barely know starts telling you about their recent breakup. What do you do?"

"Leave," I said immediately. "Fake an emergency and leave. Or hide in the bathroom. Or find the host's cat and spend the whole party with the cat."

"What if you can't leave?"

"Dissociate until it's over. Nod and make appropriate sounds while mentally reciting prime numbers or designing a categorization system for different types of pasta."

She looked at me. "Has anyone ever told you that you might be autistic?"

"I'm not autistic," I said reflexively. "I make eye contact. I understand sarcasm. Sometimes. When it's obvious. Or explained. I don't like trains." I paused. "I mean, trains are fine. The concept is elegant. The engineering is actually fascinating. Did you know the first steam locomotive–"

She was smiling slightly. "What about ADHD?"

"I'm not hyperactive," I said, while simultaneously tapping my foot, clicking my pen, and mentally rearranging the books on her shelf by height.

"Hyperactivity can be internal," she said. "Racing thoughts. Mental restlessness. The feeling that your brain has forty-seven tabs open at all times."

"Doesn't everyone's brain work like that?"

"No," she said gently. "No, it doesn't."

The Reckoning

Two weeks later, I sat in the same beige chair while she explained my results.

"You have what we call AuDHD," she said. "Autism and ADHD together. They're both clearly present, have been since childhood, and significantly impact your daily functioning."

I stared at the diagnostic report. There it was, in clinical black and white. All my contradictions explained. All my failures reframed. All my exhaustion validated.

"The autism creates a need for sameness, routine, and predictability," she explained. "The ADHD craves novelty, spontaneity, and stimulation. You've been fighting a civil war in your brain your entire life."

"So I'm not broken?"

"You're not broken. Your brain just processes things differently. You've been trying to run Windows software on a Mac operating system, then wondering why everything keeps crashing."

I wanted to cry. Or laugh. Or info-dump about operating system metaphors. Instead, I just sat there, feeling something I hadn't felt in years: hope.

"What now?" I asked.

"Now," she said, "you learn to work with your brain instead of against it. You stop trying to be neurotypical and start figuring out what works for your specific neurotype."

The Aftermath

I called my mom from the parking lot.

"I have autism and ADHD," I said, no preamble.

"Oh thank god," she said, which wasn't what I expected. "I mean, not thank god you have them, but thank god there's an answer. I've been reading about it since you mentioned the evaluation and it all makes sense. Everything makes sense now."

My sister was less surprised. "Yeah, that tracks," she said. "Remember when you alphabetized my bookshelf without asking then got distracted halfway through and left them all over my floor?"

"That was helping," I protested.

"That was the most AuDHD thing ever and we just didn't have words for it."

My dad took longer to process. "But you're smart," he kept saying, like intelligence and neurodivergence were mutually exclusive. It took time to help him understand that my brain wasn't broken or limited, just different. That all those years of struggling weren't from lack of trying but from trying to be something I'm not.

The Decision Point

The diagnosis should have felt like an ending. Question asked, answer received, mystery solved. Instead, it felt like standing at the edge of a cliff, knowing I had to jump but not knowing how to fly.

Everything I'd built – career, relationships, identity – was constructed on the foundation of masking. Now that I knew what

63

was under the mask, I had to decide: keep pretending and probably burn out again, or start over as myself and risk losing everything.

Except I'd already lost everything, hadn't I? Job, gone. Relationship, over. Friendships, faded. Health, crashed.

What was left to lose?

"I'm done," I told my reflection in my childhood bedroom mirror. The same mirror where I'd practiced "normal" facial expressions as a kid. Where I'd rehearsed conversations as a teenager. Where I'd put on masks for so many years I'd forgotten my real face.

"I'm done pretending to be neurotypical. I'm done apologizing for how my brain works. I'm done trying to fit into spaces that were never designed for me."

My reflection looked tired but also, maybe, a little bit free.

The breaking point, it turns out, wasn't a disaster.

It was a beginning.

Chapter 9: Finding the Station

The diagnosis was like getting glasses after a lifetime of squinting. Everything was still the same, but suddenly I could see it clearly. The problem was, now that I could see clearly, I realized just how much I'd been missing.

I spent the first week after diagnosis in what I can only describe as a research fugue state. Hyperfocus and special interest combined into this beautiful, terrible deep dive into everything AuDHD. I read every study, watched every video, joined every online community. I consumed information like I'd been starving for it – which, in a way, I had been.

"Stimming," I said out loud to my laptop at 3 AM, watching a video of someone flapping their hands with joy. "It's called stimming and it's normal and it's okay and I'm allowed to do it."

I flapped my hands experimentally. It felt like coming home.

The Recognition Flood

Every article, every post, every shared experience was a mirror reflecting parts of me I'd hidden for so long I'd forgotten they existed.

Executive dysfunction wasn't laziness – it was my brain literally unable to initiate tasks despite desperately wanting to do them. That thing where I'd sit for hours knowing I needed to shower, wanting to shower, completely unable to make my body move toward the shower? That had a name. It had an explanation. Other people experienced it too.

Rejection sensitive dysphoria explained why criticism felt like physical pain, why even gentle feedback could send me spiraling for days, why the thought of someone being disappointed in me was literally unbearable. It wasn't being "too sensitive" – it was my nervous system processing rejection as actual danger.

Special interests weren't weird obsessions – they were how my autistic brain found joy and made sense of the world. The intensity, the need to know everything, the info-dumping that drove people away – it was all part of how my brain sought pattern and meaning.

Time blindness wasn't irresponsibility – it was my ADHD brain's inability to feel the passage of time. Five minutes and five hours felt the same until suddenly they didn't, and I was three hours late or three hours early with no real understanding of how either happened.

"Look at this," I told my mom, shoving my laptop at her for the hundredth time that week. "This person describes exactly what happens in my brain when plans change. Exactly! Word for word what I experience but could never explain!"

She read it, eyes widening. "Oh honey. You've been dealing with all this alone?"

Not alone, exactly. But without language for it, without understanding, without knowing that millions of other people were fighting the same battles.

The Online Tribe

I found them at 2 AM on a Tuesday, three weeks into my diagnosis journey. My people. My neurotype. My tribe.

It started with Reddit, because of course it did. r/AutisticWithADHD became my homepage. Here were people describing my exact experiences, using words I'd never had, validating struggles I'd thought were personal failings.

Someone posted about "ADHD paralysis vs autism shutdown" and I read it seven times, crying because finally, finally someone understood the difference. The paralysis was wanting to do everything but being unable to start anything. The shutdown was the complete system failure when sensory and social demands exceeded capacity. I'd experienced both, sometimes simultaneously, and never had words for either.

The Discord servers were even better. Real-time conversation with people whose brains worked like mine. Where info-dumping was encouraged. Where someone could say "I'm going nonverbal but still want to hang out" and everyone understood. Where we could stim together on video calls and nobody thought it was weird.

"You're on your computer a lot lately," my dad observed, concerned.

"I found my people," I told him, not looking away from the screen where someone was explaining their color-coding system for managing both executive dysfunction and need for routine.

"Your people are online?"

"My people are everywhere," I said. "We just hadn't found each other before."

The Validation Years

Every day brought new revelations, new recognition, new validation of experiences I'd thought were unique to my broken brain.

That thing where I needed to watch the same TV show repeatedly because new shows required too much processing energy? Common AuDHD experience. The comfort of familiarity (autism) combined with brain seeking easy dopamine (ADHD).

The way I could hyperfocus for 14 hours on something interesting but couldn't maintain attention for 14 seconds on something boring? Not a character flaw. Neurological difference in dopamine regulation and attention management.

My seemingly contradictory need for routine but hatred of monotony? Classic AuDHD push-pull. My brain needed the structure to function but the novelty to stay engaged.

The sensory issues that seemed to change daily – sometimes touch was amazing, sometimes it was torture? Sensory processing differences that fluctuated based on stress, energy, and nervous system regulation.

"I'm not crazy," I kept saying, to my parents, to my sister, to my reflection, to the void. "I'm not lazy or crazy or broken. I'm autistic and ADHD and that's okay. That's actually completely okay."

My mom found me crying over a blog post about autistic joy – the pure, unfiltered happiness that comes from engaging with special interests, from stimming freely, from finding patterns and connections. I'd felt that joy but had been taught to hide it, moderate it, be embarrassed by it.

"I'm allowed to be happy in my own way," I told her through tears. "The flapping and the jumping and the excited sounds – I'm allowed to do all of it."

Learning the Language

With diagnosis came language. Beautiful, specific, validating language.

Echolalia: the repetition of sounds or phrases that felt good in my mouth. I'd done it my whole life, hidden it my whole life, been embarrassed by it my whole life. Now I knew it had a name and a purpose – self-soothing, processing, pure joy in the sensory experience of words.

Proprioception: the sense of where your body is in space. Mine was terrible, which explained why I bumped into everything, sat in weird positions, and needed heavy blankets to know where I ended and the world began.

Interoception: awareness of internal body signals. Also terrible, which explained why I'd forget to eat until I was shaking, forget to pee until it was an emergency, not notice I was cold until I was hypothermic.

Masking: the thing I'd been doing since childhood without knowing it had a name. The exhausting performance of neurotypicality that had slowly been killing me.

Spoons: the metaphor for energy that finally helped me explain why some days I could conquer the world and other days I couldn't leave bed. Limited spoons, different costs for different tasks, no reliable way to generate more.

"I need subtitles," I announced to my family, apropos of nothing.

"What?"

"Auditory processing disorder. It's why I can hear but not understand, especially with background noise. I need subtitles on everything. I'm not being difficult – my brain literally processes auditory information differently."

My dad immediately turned on subtitles. Such a small thing. Such a huge thing.

The Special Interest Inception

The beautiful irony was that AuDHD became my special interest. Learning about the thing that made me learn things the way I learned things.

I created spreadsheets tracking my sensory triggers, color-coded by type and intensity. I mapped my executive function patterns, looking for correlations with sleep, food, stress, weather. I documented my stims, categorizing them by function: happy stims, anxiety stims, thinking stims, regulation stims.

"You're studying yourself like a science project," my sister said, finding me surrounded by notebooks and charts.

"I am a science project," I told her. "I'm the experiment and the researcher and the data all at once."

The ADHD part loved the novelty of discovering new things about myself daily. The autism part loved the patterns, the categories, the systematic understanding of my own operating system. For once, both parts of my brain were pulling in the same direction.

I read about the double empathy problem – how autistics and non-autistics struggle to understand each other not because autistics lack empathy, but because we're operating with different communication styles. I read about neurodiversity, the social model of disability, the pathology paradigm versus the neurodiversity paradigm.

"It's not that I'm bad at being human," I explained to my mom. "It's that society defines 'human' in a very specific neurotypical way, then pathologizes anyone whose brain works differently."

She looked overwhelmed. "That's... a lot to think about."

"I've had 27 years of thinking I was wrong," I said. "Now I get to think about how maybe the world just wasn't built for minds like mine."

The Grief Underneath

But alongside the validation and excitement came grief. Deep, unexpected, overwhelming grief.

Grief for the child who didn't know why everything was so hard. For the teenager who thought she was broken. For the young adult who destroyed herself trying to appear normal. For all the years of unnecessary suffering that could have been avoided with earlier diagnosis.

"I'm angry," I told my therapist – a new one, specifically trained in neurodivergence. "I showed every single sign. How did nobody notice?"

"They noticed," she said gently. "They just didn't know what they were seeing. Thirty years ago, we thought autism looked like one very specific thing. Twenty years ago, we didn't understand ADHD in girls. Ten years ago, we didn't really recognize masking. You fell through the cracks of evolving understanding."

The grief came in waves. Finding old report cards that basically screamed undiagnosed AuDHD. Photos of me at social events, seeing the mask I didn't know I was wearing, the exhaustion visible even through the smile. Remembering relationships that ended because I couldn't maintain the performance.

I mourned the life I might have had with support, understanding, accommodations. The career paths closed to me because I burned out trying to be neurotypical. The relationships lost to misunderstanding and miscommunication. The years of health problems from chronic stress and masking.

"But you know now," my therapist reminded me. "That's what matters."

The Decision to Dig Deeper

Six months into knowing I was AuDHD, I decided I wanted to understand everything. Not just the surface-level "what" but the deep "why" and "how."

I started with neuroscience, hyperfocusing on brain structure and function. The differences in connectivity, neurotransmitter function, sensory processing. I learned about the intense world theory, the predictive processing differences, the default mode network variations.

71

"You're becoming an expert," my mom said, finding me surrounded by neuroscience textbooks I'd bought with my savings.

"I'm becoming myself," I corrected. "I'm learning the user manual for my own brain."

Then came the history. Learning about Hans Asperger and the Nazi connections we don't talk about enough. About how autism was first identified but misunderstood. About the refrigerator mother theory that traumatized generations. About how ADHD was thought to be childhood-only, boy-only, hyperactivity-only.

I learned about the neurodiversity movement, the self-advocacy movement, the actually autistic community fighting for acceptance over awareness. I read autistic authors, watched ADHD content creators, found scholars and activists and artists whose brains worked like mine.

"This is what representation feels like," I said to no one in particular, watching an autistic YouTuber stim while explaining special interests. "This is what it's like to see yourself reflected."

The Community Echo

The online communities became my lifeline. Not just for information, but for connection. Real, authentic connection with people who understood.

We shared wins that neurotypicals wouldn't understand. "I showered AND brushed my teeth today!" got celebrations because we knew what that took. "I made a phone call!" was met with genuine pride because phone calls were torture. "I wore jeans for three hours!" was an achievement worth acknowledging.

We shared struggles without judgment. Executive dysfunction, sensory overload, burnout, shutdown, meltdown – all met with understanding and practical advice from people who'd been there.

We shared humor that only we would find funny. Memes about object permanence ("If I can't see it, it doesn't exist, including important bills and vegetables in my fridge"). Jokes about special interests ("My Roman Empire? Actual Rome. For six months. I memorized the entire timeline of emperors"). Comics about the ADHD-autism internal argument ("We need routine!" "Routine is boring!" "But unexpected changes are scary!" "But predictability is death!").

"You're laughing at your phone a lot," my dad observed.

I showed him a meme about accidentally becoming nocturnal because time blindness and revenge bedtime procrastination combined into a perfect storm of 5 AM bedtimes.

He didn't get it. But my people did. And that was enough.

Chapter 10: Frequency Match

The diagnostic report was twelve pages long. I'd read it so many times I could recite parts from memory, but I kept returning to one line: "Clear evidence of both autism spectrum disorder and attention-deficit/hyperactivity disorder, presenting as a complex interplay of symptoms that significantly impact daily functioning."

Complex interplay. That was one way to describe the chaos in my brain.

Three months after my initial diagnosis, I decided I wanted the full picture. Not just "yes, you're AuDHD" but the complete neuropsychological workup. I wanted to understand exactly how my brain worked, where it excelled, where it struggled, and why it felt like I was constantly fighting myself.

"More testing?" my mom asked, watching me research neuropsychologists who specialized in adult neurodivergence. "Didn't you already get answers?"

"I got the headline," I told her. "Now I want the full article."

The Deep Dive Evaluation

Dr. Chen specialized in what she called "neurodivergent profiles" rather than just diagnoses. Her office wasn't beige – it was soft blues and greens with adjustable lighting and a white noise machine. She had fidgets on the table and explicitly said I could stim during our sessions.

"I'm not interested in deficits," she said during our first meeting. "I want to understand how your brain processes information, what patterns emerge, where the strengths and challenges intersect."

The testing was extensive. IQ subtests that revealed massive discrepancies – 99th percentile for pattern recognition and visual-spatial reasoning, 15th percentile for working memory and processing speed. The gap was so significant she retested certain sections to make sure.

"This is called a spiky profile," she explained, showing me a graph that looked like a mountain range. "It's very common in AuDHD. Your brain has areas of exceptional ability right next to areas of significant challenge. It's why you can seem brilliant one moment and completely lost the next."

We did sensory assessments that finally quantified what I'd always known – I was hypersensitive to light, sound, and light touch, but hyposensitive to proprioceptive and vestibular input. Translation: fluorescent lights were torture but I needed intense physical pressure to feel grounded.

The executive function testing was almost funny in how badly I failed certain parts. Object permanence, task initiation, set-shifting, time management – all significantly below average. But cognitive flexibility when interested, hyperfocus capacity, and pattern recognition – off the charts.

"Your brain is like a Ferrari engine in a golf cart chassis with bicycle brakes," Dr. Chen said, which was the most accurate description I'd ever heard.

The Validation and the Grief

The full report was forty-three pages. Forty-three pages of validation that my struggles were real, measurable, neurological.

But also forty-three pages of grief. Seeing it all written out – the executive dysfunction scores, the sensory processing differences, the social communication challenges – made it impossible to maintain any fantasy that I might wake up one day and be neurotypical.

"This is permanent," I said to Dr. Chen during our feedback session.

"Your neurotype is permanent," she agreed. "But your relationship with it isn't. Neither is your functionality. These aren't fixed limitations – they're starting points for understanding and adaptation."

She was right, but it still felt like mourning. I grieved the imaginary future where I somehow "got better" and became normal. Where I could handle fluorescent lights and last-minute plans and small talk and open offices and all the things the world expected me to handle.

"But look at this," Dr. Chen said, pointing to the strengths section of the report. "Pattern recognition in the 99th percentile. Verbal comprehension in the 95th. Fluid reasoning in the 97th when interested. These aren't consolation prizes – these are genuine cognitive gifts."

Gifts that came with costs, but gifts nonetheless.

Reframing Everything

With the full diagnostic picture, I started the process of reframing my entire life through this new lens.

That time in third grade when I had a meltdown because we had indoor recess instead of outdoor? Not bratty – autistic need for routine disrupted plus ADHD need for physical movement denied.

The friendship in high school that imploded because I forgot to respond to messages for three weeks then sent seventeen paragraphs about my current obsession? ADHD object permanence issues plus autistic info-dumping.

The job where I revolutionized their systems then forgot to come to work? Autistic pattern recognition and systematizing plus ADHD time blindness and executive dysfunction.

Every memory got recontextualized. Every failure reframed. Every quirk explained.

"It's like finding out you've been playing life on expert mode without knowing there were difficulty settings," I told my therapist.

"More like you've been playing a completely different game than everyone else but trying to follow their rules," she corrected.

The Medication Question

ADHD medication was presented as an option. Dr. Chen was careful to explain that medication was a tool, not a cure, and that with AuDHD, the response could be complicated.

"Some people find ADHD meds help with executive function but increase anxiety or sensory sensitivity," she explained. "Others find the improved focus helps them manage autistic traits better. It's very individual."

I tried Adderall first. The first day was revelatory – like someone had turned on windshield wipers in my brain. I could think one thought at a time. I could start tasks without three hours of mental preparation. I did laundry, answered emails, and made a phone call all in the same day.

"Is this how neurotypical people feel all the time?" I asked my psychiatrist.

But by day three, the side effects hit. My already-sensitive sensory system went into overdrive. Clothes felt like sandpaper. Sounds felt like physical assault. My anxiety skyrocketed. I could focus, but I was focusing on how completely overwhelming existing was.

We tried different meds, different doses, different combinations. Ritalin made me feel like a robot. Vyvanse worked for exactly four hours then dropped me off a cliff. Strattera gave me such intense nausea I couldn't function.

Eventually, we found a low dose of extended-release Adderall that helped just enough – not perfect focus, but better executive function without sensory torture. It was a compromise, like everything else in my AuDHD life.

Learning My Operating System

With diagnosis and medication sorted, I became obsessed with understanding my personal operating system. I tracked everything, looking for patterns.

I discovered that my sensory sensitivities fluctuated with my hormonal cycle. That my executive function was worst on days with barometric pressure changes. That my social battery was actually pretty large if I had enough recovery time. That certain types of cognitive tasks gave me energy while others drained me completely.

I learned that I could handle bright lights or loud sounds but not both. That I needed exactly seven hours and twenty minutes of sleep – not seven, not seven and a half. That eating the same safe foods repeatedly wasn't boring but necessary for reducing decision fatigue.

"You're turning yourself into a science experiment," my sister observed.

"I'm turning myself into a user manual," I corrected. "If I understand the inputs and outputs, I can optimize the system."

The autism part loved the data, the patterns, the systematic approach. The ADHD part loved the novelty of constant discovery and experimentation. For once, both parts were working together.

The Unmasking Process

With understanding came the terrifying prospect of unmasking. Of stopping the performance and being authentically, visibly neurodivergent.

I started small. Stimming in front of family – rocking while watching TV, flapping when excited, making my happy sounds when something pleased me. My parents tried to be supportive, though I could see the discomfort sometimes.

"It's just... different," my mom said carefully, watching me flap my hands while info-dumping about my latest special interest (the history of linguistic evolution).

"I'm different," I reminded her. "You've known that for 27 years. Now you're just seeing it instead of me hiding it."

Next came public spaces. Using stim toys in waiting rooms. Wearing noise-canceling headphones in stores. Taking breaks when overwhelmed instead of pushing through. Each small act of visibility felt simultaneously terrifying and liberating.

The first time I told someone "I'm autistic and ADHD" out loud, my heart was pounding so hard I thought I might pass out. It was just the barista at my local coffee shop, explaining why I needed to know all the ingredients in their seasonal drink, but it felt monumental.

"Oh cool, my brother's autistic too," she said, and that was it. The world didn't end. I didn't spontaneously combust. I just got my coffee with full ingredient knowledge and went about my day.

Finding My Frequency

The diagnosis journey wasn't just about understanding my challenges – it was about discovering that my frequency, while different, was completely valid.

I found that when I stopped fighting my brain's natural patterns, things got easier. Not easy, but easier. When I worked with my hyperfocus instead of against it, I could accomplish incredible things. When I honored my sensory needs instead of pushing through, I had more energy. When I let myself stim, my anxiety decreased.

I started building a life that matched my frequency instead of trying to tune into everyone else's.

I switched to working freelance, choosing projects that interested me and working during my peak focus hours (2 AM to 6 AM, it turned out). I created elaborate organizational systems that satisfied my autism need for order while having enough flexibility for my ADHD need for spontaneity.

I decorated my space in ways that made my brain happy – fairy lights instead of overhead lighting, soft textures everywhere, a designated pacing path, visual schedules that I could completely ignore when executive function failed.

"It looks like a sensory room crossed with a command center," my sister said, visiting my newly optimized space.

"It looks like my brain made physical," I said. "And that's exactly what I need."

The Relief of Recognition

The biggest relief wasn't just understanding myself – it was being understood by others who operated on similar frequencies.

In online spaces, I could say "I'm having an ADHD paralysis day but also autism needs routine met so I'm stuck in a loop of distress" and people would just get it. No explanation needed. No justification required.

I found local neurodivergent meet-ups where everyone wore headphones or sunglasses indoors and nobody questioned it. Where info-dumping was encouraged. Where stimming was so normal it was weird not to do it.

"These are your people?" my mom asked, picking me up from a meet-up where we'd spent three hours categorizing types of clouds while simultaneously having four different conversations.

"These are my people," I confirmed. "My frequency matches theirs."

The diagnosis hadn't changed who I was. I'd always been AuDHD. But now I had words for it, understanding of it, and most importantly, a community of others whose brains worked the same beautiful, chaotic, contradictory way.

I was still the same person who needed routine but craved novelty, who could hyperfocus for hours but couldn't remember to eat, who felt everything too much and not enough all at once.

But now I knew why. Now I had language. Now I had permission to be exactly who I'd always been.

The static was clearing. My frequency was coming through clear and strong.

And for the first time in my life, I didn't want to change the channel.

Chapter 11: Playback

The photo album was a time capsule of masks I didn't know I'd been wearing.

Six months into my diagnosis journey, I sat on my bedroom floor surrounded by decades of photos, report cards, birthday cards, and home videos. My mom had kept everything – every school report, every teacher's note, every "concerned" letter home. She'd brought them out when I asked, tears in her eyes.

"I saved them because I always felt like someday they'd make sense," she said. "Like eventually we'd understand what we were seeing."

Now we did. And the evidence had been there all along.

The Childhood Receipts

Here was five-year-old me at a birthday party, pressed against a wall while chaos swirled around. The photo was supposed to capture "fun," but all I could see was the overwhelm in my tiny face, the way my hands were clenched, the forced smile that didn't reach my eyes.

"You always did that," my mom said, looking over my shoulder. "Found a wall or corner at every event. We thought you were just shy."

Shy. The neurotypical explanation for autistic social overwhelm.

Report card after report card told the same story in different words. "Extremely bright but inconsistent." "Needs to apply herself more consistently." "Capable of exceptional work when interested." "Has difficulty with transitions." "Would benefit from more social interaction with peers."

One teacher had written an entire paragraph that, in retrospect, was basically describing executive dysfunction in perfect detail without having the words for it: "She seems to understand concepts completely but cannot demonstrate this knowledge consistently. She'll complete work brilliantly one day then seem unable to start the same type of task the next. It's as if her ability to access her own knowledge varies day to day."

"I wanted to get you tested," my mom admitted. "But for what? You were smart, you had some friends, you weren't failing. Nobody could tell me what was 'wrong,' just that something was different."

The Missing Pieces

The home videos were the worst. Or best. Depending on how you looked at it.

There I was, age seven, lining up my entire toy collection by size, sub-sorted by color, while narrating the classification system to my exhausted-looking father. The autism was right there – the need for order, the systematic categorization, the monologuing about my special interest.

But then the video continued, and there I was five minutes later, abandoning the entire project mid-sort because I'd seen a butterfly outside. The ADHD was right there too – the instant distraction, the abandoned project, the inability to return to the task despite being genuinely upset about the unfinished sorting.

"You did that constantly," my dad said, watching with me. "Start these elaborate organizational projects then abandon them halfway through. We never understood why you'd get so upset about not finishing things you'd chosen to stop doing."

Because I hadn't chosen. My ADHD brain had hijacked my autism brain mid-task, and both parts were distressed about it.

Another video: my ninth birthday. I'd asked for a small family dinner. Just us, my safe foods, my routine. Instead, surprise! Extended family, loud cousins, foods I couldn't eat, and me having what was clearly an autistic meltdown that everyone attributed to being "overtired" and "overexcited."

"We thought we were making you happy," my mom said quietly. "You seemed so isolated. We wanted you to have a normal birthday."

Normal. The word that had haunted my entire childhood. The standard I could never quite reach no matter how hard I tried.

The Teen Years Archive

High school was documented in excruciating detail thanks to early social media. Facebook memories kept popping up, each one a masterclass in masking.

Status updates that were clearly scripted attempts at normal teen communication. Photos where I was always slightly apart from the group, mimicking their poses a beat too late. Comments on friends' posts that were just slightly off – too formal, too intense, or completely missing the social cues.

My journal from that time was painful to read. Page after page of trying to decode social interactions, creating rules and scripts for different situations. "When someone says 'how are you,' they don't want real answer. Say 'fine, you?' and move on." "Laugh when others laugh, even if you don't understand why." "Don't talk about special interests unless directly asked, and even then, keep it under two minutes."

I'd written actual scripts for phone calls. Drawings of facial expressions with labels. Detailed notes about what topics were acceptable with which people. It was like reading the anthropological field notes of an alien trying to pass as human.

"Did you know?" I asked my sister, who'd been there through all of it.

"I knew you were different," she said carefully. "But I thought you were just... you. Quirky. Intense. I didn't know you were struggling so much. You hid it really well."

Too well. So well that even I hadn't fully understood how much I was masking.

The College Collapse Documentation

My college years were preserved in emails, medical records, and academic transcripts that told a story of gradual system failure.

Freshman year: Dean's list first semester, academic probation second semester. The emails from professors confused by my "inconsistent performance" and "unusual pattern of strengths and challenges."

Sophomore year: Medical leave for "anxiety and depression" that was actually autistic burnout, but nobody knew to call it that.

Junior year: Switching majors for the third time, each change corresponding to a new special interest that my ADHD brain had latched onto with desperate intensity.

Senior year: The gradual deterioration visible in increasingly erratic emails, missed assignments despite understanding the material, and health center visits for stress-related physical symptoms.

"I have your final thesis here," my mom said, pulling out a bound document. "You got an A+. The professor said it was graduate-level work."

I remembered that thesis. Written in a 72-hour hyperfocus fugue, fueled by a special interest intersection that had made my brain light up like fireworks. It was brilliant. It was also written instead of attending to any other responsibilities for weeks, and I'd collapsed completely afterward.

Classic AuDHD: capable of extraordinary things when the conditions aligned, completely non-functional when they didn't.

The Employment Evidence

My work history was filed in a folder labeled "Jobs" in my mom's neat handwriting. Performance reviews that swung between "exceptional" and "needs improvement," sometimes in the same document.

One manager had written: "She revolutionized our filing system but seems unable to follow the dress code consistently. She remembers every detail from meetings months ago but forgets to submit weekly reports. She's either the best employee we've ever had or completely checked out, with no middle ground."

There were exit interviews where I'd tried to explain why I was leaving without having the words. "The environment is too... much." "I need more... flexibility but also structure?" "The lights make it hard to think."

Recommendation letters that all said variations of the same thing: "When she's on, she's exceptional. Creative, dedicated, innovative. But there are reliability concerns."

Reliability. Because showing up when your sensory system is overloaded, your executive function is offline, and you're in autistic shutdown isn't reliable. Because maintaining consistent performance when your brain operates in extremes isn't reliable. Because being neurotypical in a neurotypical world is reliable, and I couldn't do that.

The Relationship Wreckage

The hardest box to go through was relationships. Cards, photos, messages from people who'd tried to love me but couldn't understand me.

"You're so hot and cold," one ex had written. "I never know which version of you I'm going to get."

"It's like you forget I exist when I'm not right in front of you," another had said.

"You care more about your hobbies than people," from a friend who'd gotten tired of competing with my special interests.

Each criticism had felt like a character flaw at the time. Now I could see the neurological patterns. Object permanence issues. Emotional dysregulation. Special interest intensity. Sensory overwhelm affecting emotional availability.

There were photos from social events where I was clearly masking so hard it was painful to see. The tension in my shoulders, the forced expressions, the way I was always holding something (drink, phone, anything) to have something to do with my hands.

"You looked happy," my mom said about one photo from a family wedding.

"I was performing happy," I corrected. "Inside, I was calculating how many minutes until I could leave without being rude."

The Reframe Revolution

With each piece of evidence, each memory recontextualized, I felt both vindicated and angry.

Vindicated because I hadn't been lazy, crazy, or broken. Every struggle had a neurological basis. Every "failure" was actually my brain operating exactly as it was designed to, just in a world not designed for it.

Angry because the signs had been there. All of them. Every single diagnostic criterion, displayed consistently for decades. But because I could speak, make eye contact (however briefly), and had learned to mask effectively, nobody thought to look deeper.

"How did everyone miss this?" I asked my therapist, spreading out the evidence of a lifetime of undiagnosed neurodivergence.

"The same way you missed it," she said gently. "We only see what we know to look for. Thirty years ago, we didn't know autism could look like you. Twenty years ago, we didn't know ADHD in girls presented differently. Ten years ago, we didn't understand masking. You were a puzzle before we had all the pieces."

The Grief and the Grace

Looking at it all – the photos, the reports, the evidence of decades of struggle – the grief hit in waves.

Grief for the little girl who thought she was broken. For the teenager who tried so hard to be normal. For the young adult who destroyed herself trying to fit a neurotypical mold. For all the years of unnecessary pain that could have been avoided with understanding and support.

But also, surprisingly, grace. Grace for my parents, who did their best with the information they had. Grace for my teachers, who saw something different but didn't have words for it. Grace for friends and partners who tried to understand but couldn't bridge the neurotype gap. Grace for younger me, who survived without a manual, without words, without understanding.

"You were so strong," my mom said, crying as we looked through everything. "You fought so hard, all alone, not even knowing what you were fighting."

"I'm not fighting anymore," I told her. "Now I'm understanding. Now I'm accepting. Now I'm rebuilding with the right blueprints."

The Integration Begins

The playback wasn't just about grieving the past – it was about integrating it into my present understanding.

Every memory reframed became a piece of evidence that yes, I'd always been autistic. Yes, I'd always had ADHD. No, I hadn't suddenly become neurodivergent at 27. I'd been neurodivergent since birth, just unrecognized and unsupported.

This mattered because imposter syndrome was real. Days when I wondered if I was making it all up, if I was just looking for excuses, if maybe I really was just lazy and weird. The evidence reminded me: no, this is real, this has always been real, and now I have words for it.

I created a new photo album. Same photos, but with new captions. "First day of school – sensory overload visible." "Birthday party – autistic shutdown in progress." "College graduation – peak masking achieved at enormous cost."

Not to dwell on the past, but to honor it. To acknowledge that little girl, that teenager, that young adult who did their absolute best with a brain they didn't understand in a world that wasn't built for them.

"You're rewriting your history," my sister observed.

"I'm writing it accurately for the first time," I corrected. "The story was always there. I just have the right language for it now."

The playback was complete. Now it was time to record something new. Something authentic. Something unmasked.

Something truly me.

Chapter 12: Adjusting the Equalizer

The first time I stimmed in public on purpose, I thought I was going to throw up from anxiety.

It was just hand-flapping. Just my hands moving in the way they'd always wanted to move, the way I'd trained them not to move for twenty-seven years. I was in Target, overwhelmed by the fluorescent lights and decision fatigue of choosing laundry detergent, and instead of white-knuckling through it like always, I let my hands flap.

For maybe three seconds.

Then I shoved them in my pockets and speed-walked to my car, convinced everyone was staring, judging, knowing.

Nobody had even noticed.

The Unmasking Experiment

Unmasking, I learned, wasn't like taking off a costume. It was more like archaeological excavation – carefully removing layers of learned behavior to find out what was actually underneath, not always sure if what you're finding is original or just another, older mask.

I started with safe spaces. My bedroom became a mask-free zone where I could rock while reading, make my weird happy sounds, eat foods in the "wrong" order, and line things up obsessively without judgment. It felt like learning to breathe with my whole lungs instead of just the top third.

"You seem different," my mom said, finding me eating lunch (cereal for lunch was perfectly valid) while rocking and organizing my rock collection by both color AND geological classification simultaneously.

"I'm the same," I told her. "I'm just not hiding it anymore."

The look on her face was complicated – relief mixed with grief mixed with something that might have been recognition. Like she was seeing echoes of the child I'd been before I learned to perform normal.

Next came family spaces. Stimming while watching TV. Info-dumping without apology. Asking for the lights to be dimmed without elaborate justification. Using my noise-canceling headphones at family dinners when the overlapping conversations became too much.

"Is this... permanent?" my dad asked, watching me flap my hands during an exciting part of a movie.

"This is me," I said. "It was always me. I was just hiding it before."

The Mask Inventory

My therapist suggested I inventory my masks – figure out which ones were protective and necessary versus which ones were just exhausting performance.

Professional Mask: Some parts needed to stay. Being able to communicate with neurotypical colleagues, meet deadlines, maintain basic hygiene standards – these weren't betrayals of my neurodivergent self. But the parts where I pretended to care about office small talk, forced myself to work in environments that caused sensory pain, and hidden all my coping mechanisms? Those could go.

Social Mask: The constant performance of neurotypical social interest was killing me. But basic kindness, respect for boundaries, reciprocal communication when I had the spoons for it – those weren't masks, they were just being a decent human.

Family Mask: This was the hardest to parse. How much of how I behaved around family was masking versus how much was just... being part of a family? The hiding of stims, definitely masking. But moderating info-dumping so others could also speak? That felt more like accommodation than betrayal.

"Think of it like code-switching," my therapist said. "Everyone adjusts their behavior for different contexts. The problem is when the adjustment requires you to suppress fundamental aspects of your neurology."

The Disclosure Dilemma

Deciding who to tell, when to tell, and how much to tell became its own exhausting equation.

At the grocery store, when overwhelmed, I didn't owe anyone an explanation for wearing headphones. But at the dentist, explaining my sensory issues got me accommodations that made the experience bearable – dimmed lights, no music, permission to stim, breaks when needed.

"I'm autistic and have sensory processing differences" became a key that unlocked accommodations I didn't know existed. Suddenly, medical professionals were willing to adjust their approach. The DMV let me wait in a quiet area. The hair salon turned off the blow dryers between clients.

But disclosure also brought risks. The landlord who suddenly found reasons to not renew my lease after learning I was autistic. The potential employer whose enthusiasm evaporated when I asked about accommodation policies. The acquaintance who started speaking to me like I was a child after disclosure.

I developed a disclosure flowchart:

- Will disclosure improve the situation? If no, don't disclose.
- Is this person safe? If unknown, proceed with caution.
- Do I have the energy for potential education? If no, maybe later.
- Is this a one-time interaction or ongoing relationship? One-time rarely worth it.

"You shouldn't have to calculate all this," my therapist said.

"No," I agreed. "But the world isn't where it should be yet. Until it is, I have to be strategic about vulnerability."

The Professional Unmasking

Work was where unmasking felt most dangerous. I'd built my entire professional reputation on being able to perform neurotypicality. Now I had to figure out how to be authentically neurodivergent while still being employable.

I started freelancing, which gave me control over my environment. I could work at 3 AM when my brain was most functional. I could pace while thinking without anyone commenting. I could take sensory breaks without permission.

But client interactions still required navigation. I started being more honest, within reason.

"I process information better in writing – could you send that in an email?"

"I work best with clear, explicit expectations. Could we document the specific deliverables?"

"I have some auditory processing challenges. Could we use video calls with captions?"

Most clients didn't care as long as the work got done. Some were confused but adaptable. A few were actively accommodating, even appreciative of the clear communication.

One client, after I explained why I needed deadline flexibility around my executive function patterns, said, "Oh thank god, someone who actually explains their needs instead of just mysteriously missing deadlines."

The Energy Economics

Unmasking, I discovered, wasn't universally energy-saving. Sometimes being authentically neurodivergent took more energy than masking, just different energy.

Masking was exhausting in a soul-crushing, identity-erasing way. But it was also familiar. I knew those scripts, those performances. They were depleting but predictable.

Being openly neurodivergent meant constant micro-decisions. Stim or suppress? Disclose or deflect? Accommodate or advocate? Each choice required conscious thought in a way that automatic masking hadn't.

"It's like learning to walk again," I told my therapist. "I know it'll eventually be easier, but right now every step requires conscious thought."

There were also energy costs to other people's reactions. The stares when I stimmed in public. The confusion when I communicated directly instead of with neurotypical subtext. The exhaustion of educating well-meaning but clueless people.

But there were energy gains too. Not suppressing stims meant less anxiety. Honoring sensory needs meant fewer meltdowns. Working with my executive function patterns instead of against them meant actually completing projects.

Finding the Balance

The goal, I realized, wasn't to never mask. It was to mask consciously, strategically, and only when necessary.

Job interview? Yeah, some masking required. But I could unmask gradually once hired and establish myself.

Doctor's appointment? Minimal masking, maximum advocacy for my needs.

Family gathering? Moderate masking for group harmony, but with planned breaks to unmask privately.

Grocery shopping? No masking needed beyond basic social politeness.

Home alone or with safe people? No masking at all.

I thought of it like adjusting an audio equalizer – different settings for different environments, but always maintaining the core frequency that was me.

"You're code-switching," my sister observed, watching me modulate between contexts. "Like bilingual people do with languages."

"Except I'm switching between neurotypes," I said. "And one of them isn't really mine, I just learned to mimic it for survival."

The Accommodation Revolution

The biggest revelation was discovering how many accommodations I could create for myself once I stopped pretending I didn't need them.

Meal planning was executive function hell, so I ate the same five safe foods on rotation and stopped apologizing for it. Grocery shopping was sensory hell, so I did pickup orders and stopped feeling guilty about not being "normal." Phone calls were special torture, so I moved everything possible to text or email and stopped forcing myself through unnecessary verbal communication.

I bought loop earplugs for restaurants, tinted glasses for fluorescent lights, and a collection of stim toys I actually used instead of hiding. I created visual schedules even though I was an adult because my time blindness didn't care about my age. I set seventeen alarms for everything because ADHD doesn't respect important appointments.

"Isn't all this... a lot?" my mom asked, watching me put on tinted glasses, loop earplugs, and compression clothing before leaving the house.

"Living in sensory pain was a lot," I told her. "This is nothing compared to that."

The Relationship Renegotiation

Unmasking meant renegotiating every relationship in my life.

Some friends were confused but adapted. "Oh, this explains so much," became a common refrain, usually followed by questions and genuine attempts to understand.

Some friends revealed themselves to also be masking neurodivergents. My unmasking gave them permission to unmask too, and suddenly relationships that had been surface-level became deeply authentic.

Some friends couldn't handle it. The friend who said stimming made her uncomfortable. The one who got angry when I couldn't handle plan changes. The ones who wanted the performed version of me, not the real one.

"You've changed," they said.

"I've stopped pretending," I corrected.

The relationships that survived became stronger. Based on actual me, not performed me. It was terrifying and beautiful and worth every lost connection that had only ever been with my mask anyway.

The Ongoing Calibration

Six months into conscious unmasking, I was still calibrating. Still adjusting the equalizer, finding the balance between authentic existence and social survival.

Some days I overcompensated, being aggressively neurodivergent in ways that weren't actually authentic, just reactive. Other days old masking habits snuck back in, and I'd realize hours later that I'd been suppressing stims or ignoring sensory needs.

"It's a process," my therapist reminded me. "You're unlearning twenty-seven years of conditioning. Be patient with yourself."

But patience was hard when every day felt like conscious performance, just in reverse. Instead of consciously performing neurotypicality, I was consciously performing authentic neurodivergence, which somehow also felt like performance.

"When does it become natural?" I asked her.

"When you stop thinking of it as performance at all," she said. "When it's just... being."

I wasn't there yet. But for the first time, I could imagine it. A life where my hands flapped when I was happy without thought or shame. Where I honored my sensory needs without elaborate justification. Where I communicated in my natural direct way without constant translation.

Where the equalizer wasn't about adjusting myself for the world, but about finding the settings where I could hear my own frequency clearly.

The static was clearing. The signal was coming through.

I just had to keep adjusting until I found the perfect balance – not between masking and unmasking, but between surviving and thriving.

Between existing and living.

Between performing life and actually living it.

Chapter 13: Stereo Sound

The revelation came at 2 AM on a Tuesday, which was pretty on-brand for my brain.

I was simultaneously researching the history of Byzantine architecture (special interest number 847) while writing code for a client project, when suddenly both sides of my brain aligned. The pattern recognition from autism was identifying structural similarities between Byzantine domes and database architecture, while the ADHD was making creative leaps between completely unrelated concepts.

The result? A database visualization system inspired by sixth-century architectural principles that was both brilliantly functional and completely bizarre.

"This is either genius or insane," the client said when I presented it.

"Both," I told them. "That's kind of my thing."

The Synthesis Discovery

For twenty-eight years, I'd thought of my autism and ADHD as opposing forces locked in eternal combat. Order versus chaos. Routine versus novelty. Focus versus distraction. But what if they weren't opposites? What if they were complementary frequencies that, when properly aligned, created something neither could achieve alone?

The autism gave me pattern recognition, systematic thinking, and the ability to hold vast amounts of information in organized mental structures. The ADHD gave me creative leaps, novel connections, and the ability to see possibilities others missed. Together, they

100

created a kind of cognitive stereo sound – full, rich, dimensional thinking that was more than the sum of its parts.

I started paying attention to when the alignment happened naturally:

- When a new interest (ADHD) became a special interest (autism)
- When systematic analysis (autism) led to creative innovation (ADHD)
- When hyperfocus (ADHD) met pattern recognition (autism)
- When routine (autism) included variety (ADHD)

"Your brain isn't broken," Dr. Chen said when I shared this discovery. "It's just operating on a different frequency. And sometimes, those frequencies create harmonics."

The Strengths Inventory

I made a list. Not of deficits this time, but of the actual advantages of my AuDHD brain:

Pattern Recognition on Steroids: I could see patterns others missed, connections between disparate things, systems within chaos. The autism identified the patterns; the ADHD connected them across domains.

Hyperfocus Superpowers: When interest aligned with importance, I could achieve in hours what took others days. The ADHD provided the intense focus; the autism provided the systematic approach.

Creative Problem-Solving: My inability to think in typical ways meant I solved problems in atypical ways. The autism analyzed every component; the ADHD recombined them in novel configurations.

Information Processing: I could hold enormous amounts of information in my head, see it from multiple angles simultaneously, and synthesize it in unique ways. Autism organized it; ADHD played with it.

Intensity and Passion: When something captured both aspects of my brain, my enthusiasm was infectious. The autism brought depth; the ADHD brought energy.

"You're not listing accommodations," my therapist noted. "You're listing superpowers."

"Same thing," I said. "They're superpowers when properly channeled, disabilities when forced into neurotypical frameworks."

The Professional Pivot

Armed with this understanding, I completely restructured my work life.

Instead of trying to fit into traditional employment, I created a consulting niche that played to my exact strengths: pattern analysis and creative solution design for complex systems. Basically, companies hired me to look at their problems with my weird brain and see solutions their neurotypical employees couldn't see.

"We need someone who thinks outside the box," one client said.

"I don't even know where the box is," I told them. "I think in dodecahedrons."

They laughed, thinking I was joking. I wasn't. But my dodecahedral thinking solved their problem in ways their box-thinking couldn't.

I scheduled my work around my brain patterns. Deep analysis during autism-dominant morning hours. Creative synthesis during ADHD-dominant afternoon chaos. Administrative tasks during the rare moments when both cooperated. Nothing during burnout periods, which I learned to predict and plan for.

"You can't just... not work when your brain doesn't want to," my dad said, still stuck in traditional employment thinking.

"Watch me," I said, showing him my income from working with my brain instead of against it – more than I'd ever made in traditional employment while working half the hours.

The Creative Explosion

When I stopped trying to separate my autism and ADHD, my creativity exploded in ways I hadn't imagined possible.

I started creating art that was simultaneously obsessively detailed (autism) and wildly creative (ADHD). Intricate patterns that broke their own rules. Systematic chaos. Organized randomness. Each piece took hundreds of hours of hyperfocused work, combining technical precision with creative abandon.

"This makes no sense," someone said at my first gallery showing. "It's too organized to be abstract but too chaotic to be structured."

"Welcome to my brain," I said.

The pieces sold out.

I started writing – not just writing, but creating these complex, interconnected story universes that required massive organizational systems (autism) but also creative innovation (ADHD). Spreadsheets of character details combined with random plot tangents that somehow worked.

Music became three-dimensional. I could hear all the layers separately and together, identify patterns while appreciating chaos, understand structure while enjoying improvisation. The autism analyzed; the ADHD synthesized; together they created this rich, full experience that made me cry from pure sensory joy.

Building the Right Environment

Creating a life that worked with both aspects meant designing everything around their intersection points.

My living space became a controlled chaos – organized zones for autism comfort, creative mess zones for ADHD stimulation. Rigid morning routines that included variety. Meal plans that were consistent but not identical. Exercise that was scheduled but varied in type.

I set up work systems that satisfied both: project management software with color-coding and tags (autism) but flexible deadlines and multiple concurrent projects (ADHD). Communication templates for efficiency (autism) but freedom to diverge when inspired (ADHD).

"Your apartment looks like it was decorated by two different people," my sister observed.

"It was," I said. "Both of them are me."

The Synergy Sessions

I discovered that I could intentionally create conditions where both aspects aligned.

New learning in systematic frameworks sparked both. Taking online courses that were structured (autism) but on new topics (ADHD). Learning languages through pattern recognition (autism) but multiple languages simultaneously (ADHD).

Physical activities that required both precision and creativity: rock climbing (planned routes but adaptive movement), martial arts (structured forms but dynamic application), dance (choreographed steps but interpretive expression).

Projects that evolved through phases: research phase (autism-dominant), synthesis phase (both active), creative phase (ADHD-dominant), refinement phase (autism-dominant again).

"You're hacking your own brain," my therapist said, impressed.

"I'm working with its actual design instead of against it," I corrected.

The Communication Bridge

The real breakthrough was learning to communicate using both aspects as a bridge to neurotypical understanding.

The autism could organize and structure my thoughts in ways neurotypicals could follow. The ADHD could add energy and engagement that held their attention. Together, I could translate my neurodivergent experience into neurotypical language without losing authenticity.

I started giving presentations about neurodiversity, using my systematic understanding to educate and my creative energy to engage. The autism provided accuracy; the ADHD provided accessibility.

"You make it make sense," an attendee said after one talk. "Like, I finally understand how my kid's brain might work."

That became my new professional focus – translation. Being a bridge between neurotypes. Using my stereo sound to help others hear frequencies they couldn't access alone.

The Integration Celebration

The day I truly felt the integration was ordinary and extraordinary.

I was working on a complex data visualization project, my autism brain creating elaborate organizational systems while my ADHD brain kept finding new patterns to explore. I was stimming freely – rocking in my chair, fidgeting with thinking putty, making happy sounds when patterns aligned. Music played at exactly the right volume, my fairy lights provided perfect lighting, and I was eating safe foods in whatever order felt right.

Both aspects of my brain were fully engaged, fully satisfied, working together instead of against each other. The hyperfocus was structured. The structure was creative. The patterns had chaos. The chaos had patterns.

"This," I said out loud to no one, "this is what I'm supposed to feel like."

Not normal. Not neurotypical. Not fixed or cured or overcoming anything.

Just authentically, completely, unapologetically AuDHD.

My phone buzzed with a client message: "The solution you designed is unlike anything we've seen, but it works perfectly. How did you even think of this?"

"Stereo sound," I typed back, knowing they wouldn't understand but not caring.

My brain wasn't broken. It was broadcasting in stereo, and I'd finally figured out how to tune both channels simultaneously.

Chapter 14: Resonance

The first time I met another AuDHD person in real life, we talked for six hours straight.

Not small talk. Real talk. We info-dumped without apology, interrupted each other constantly but somehow never lost the thread, switched topics every twelve seconds while somehow covering everything in depth, and stimmed the entire time without either of us mentioning it.

"Is this what friendship is supposed to feel like?" I asked her as we parted ways at 2 AM, both of us energized rather than drained.

"I don't know," she said, flapping her hands excitedly. "But if it is, I've been doing it wrong for thirty years."

Her name was Jordan, and she became the first pillar in what would become my actually authentic support network.

Building the Neurodivergent Network

After Jordan, I started actively seeking out neurodivergent connections. Not just online anymore, but in person, building real relationships with people whose brains worked like mine.

There was Marcus, autistic with anxiety, who understood the need for scripts and schedules and showed me how he'd built an entire life that looked "normal" from the outside but was actually perfectly accommodated for his brain.

There was Sage, ADHD with suspected autism, who taught me about rejection sensitive dysphoria by crying with me about it for three hours, then immediately pivoting to excited info-dumping about their special interest in mushroom cultivation.

There was River, diagnosed AuDHD at 45, who became my mentor in learning to unmask professionally while still maintaining income. They'd built a successful consulting business by being aggressively authentic – stimming in client meetings, setting boundaries about communication preferences, and refusing to apologize for their brain.

"The right clients don't care if you're weird if you're good," River told me. "And we're very, very good at what we do when we're allowed to do it our way."

The Family Education Project

Building authentic relationships with new people was one thing. Rebuilding relationships with family was another.

I created what I called the Family Education Project – a systematic (autism) but creative (ADHD) approach to helping my family understand my neurotype.

I started with articles, sending one every week with key points highlighted. "This explains why I can't handle restaurants." "This describes what shutdown feels like." "This is why I need routine but also novelty."

"It's a lot of information," my mom said after week three.

"It's twenty-eight years of information compressed into weekly emails," I pointed out. "You're getting the CliffsNotes version of my entire existence."

Then came practical demonstrations. I brought my family to a sensory store, had them wear noise-amplifying headphones and scratchy shirts while trying to have a conversation under fluorescent lights.

"I feel like I'm going to scream," my dad said after five minutes.

"Welcome to my everyday experience," I told him. "Except I can't take the headphones off."

My sister was the quickest study. She started dimming lights without being asked, texting instead of calling, and learning to recognize when I was approaching overload before I did.

"You're pattern recognition is rubbing off on me," she joked, but it wasn't really a joke. She was learning to read me without the mask, and I was learning to let myself be read.

The Partner Paradox

Dating while openly neurodivergent was terrifying and liberating in equal measure.

I put it right in my dating profile: "AuDHD. If you don't know what that means, we're probably not compatible." It filtered out 90% of matches. Good.

The remaining 10% fell into categories:

- Other neurodivergents looking for someone who'd understand
- Neurotypicals who'd dated neurodivergents before
- People who fetishized neurodivergence (blocked immediately)
- The curious but educable

Alex (different Alex) was in the second category. They'd dated an autistic person before, understood stimming, sensory issues, and info-dumping. But they'd never experienced the AuDHD contradiction.

"So you need routine but hate monotony?" they asked on our first date.

"Yes."

"And you can hyperfocus for twelve hours but can't remember if you ate lunch?"

"Correct."

"And you need deep pressure but light touch makes you want to crawl out of your skin?"

"You're getting it!"

They laughed. "You're like... a walking paradox."

"I prefer 'neurologically complex,'" I said, and they laughed again, but not at me. With me. Important difference.

The Advocacy Evolution

As I built authentic relationships, I found myself naturally becoming an advocate. Not just for myself, but for neurodivergent understanding in general.

It started small. Correcting misconceptions when I heard them. "Actually, autism isn't a spectrum from 'less' to 'more' autistic. It's more like a color wheel of different traits and intensities."

Then bigger. Speaking at local organizations about neurodiversity in the workplace. Writing articles about the intersection of autism and ADHD. Consulting with companies on neurodivergent accommodation.

"You're becoming an activist," Jordan said, watching me prepare for another presentation.

"I'm becoming visible," I corrected. "And visibility is activism when you're not supposed to exist."

Because that was the thing – AuDHD people weren't supposed to exist in the public imagination. We were supposed to be either autistic OR ADHD, either successful OR struggling, either independent OR needing support. The both/and of our existence challenged neat categories.

The Support Network Dynamics

My support network became this beautiful, chaotic mesh of different neurotypes and communication styles.

We had a group chat that was pure chaos – seventeen concurrent conversations, no one finishing a thought, everyone understanding perfectly. We had parallel play hangouts where we'd all do our own things in the same space, occasionally sharing random thoughts. We had info-dump sessions where everyone got twenty minutes to monologue about their current special interest without interruption.

"This is the weirdest friend group I've ever seen," my neurotypical cousin said, observing one of our gatherings.

"Weird by whose standards?" I asked.

She thought about it. "Fair point."

We supported each other in ways neurotypical friends never had. Body doubling for tasks that required executive function. Sensory-safe house parties with adjustable lighting and quiet spaces. Reminder texts for important things because we all struggled with time blindness. Celebration of achievements neurotypicals wouldn't understand – "I made three phone calls today!" was met with genuine pride and understanding of what that took.

The Professional Network Effect

As I became more open about my neurotype professionally, something unexpected happened: other neurodivergent professionals started finding me.

Soon I had a network of AuDHD, autistic, ADHD, and otherwise neurodivergent professionals who referred clients to each other, collaborated on projects, and created our own little economy of accommodation and understanding.

We communicated primarily through voice messages (for those who hated typing) or text (for those who hated phone calls). We had meetings with cameras optional, stimming encouraged, and info-dumping expected. We set deadlines with buffer time built in for executive dysfunction. We celebrated hyperfocus achievements and supported each other through burnout.

"You've created your own business culture," one neurotypical client observed.

"We've created a business culture that works for our brains," I corrected. "Turns out, when you accommodate neurodivergence, you get exceptional results."

The Relationship Reconstruction

Six months into dating Alex, I had my first full meltdown in front of them.

It wasn't planned. Meltdowns never are. But the restaurant was louder than expected, they'd changed the menu without warning, the lights were wrong, my clothes suddenly felt like sandpaper, and my nervous system just... gave up.

I stimmed violently, couldn't speak, cried from pure overload. Full autism meltdown while my ADHD brain scattered in seventeen directions trying to find an escape route.

Alex didn't try to fix it. Didn't get embarrassed. Didn't make it about them. They just got me out of there, drove me home in silence, and waited.

"I'm sorry," I said when I could speak again.

"For what?" they asked. "For having a neurological response to sensory overload? That's like apologizing for bleeding when you're cut."

That's when I knew this relationship was different. They saw me, not despite my neurodivergence but including it. All of it.

The Self-Acceptance Process

Building authentic relationships forced me to confront the last frontier: actually accepting myself.

I could advocate for neurodiversity, educate others, build accommodating structures, but deep down, part of me still believed I was broken. Still apologized for existing. Still felt like a burden.

"You're the harshest on yourself," Jordan observed. "You accept everyone else's neurodivergence but treat yours like a personal failing."

She was right. I gave others grace I denied myself. Celebrated their achievements while minimizing mine. Validated their struggles while calling mine weakness.

The self-acceptance didn't come all at once. It came in moments:

- Stimming in public without shame
- Asking for accommodations without apology
- Setting boundaries without justification
- Celebrating my brain instead of despite it
- Choosing authenticity over acceptance

"I'm not broken," I said to my reflection one morning, and for the first time, I believed it.

The Resonance Reality

True resonance, I learned, wasn't about finding people exactly like me. It was about finding people who vibrated at compatible frequencies. Whose differences harmonized with mine. Whose understanding came not from sameness but from mutual respect for different ways of being.

My support network became this beautiful symphony of different neurotypes, all playing our own instruments but creating music together. We weren't trying to match each other's frequencies – we were creating harmony from diversity.

"Your whole life has changed," my mom observed, watching me prepare for a neurodivergent community gathering I was hosting.

"My life is the same," I told her. "I just have people who understand it now."

The resonance wasn't just with others. It was with myself. For the first time, all my parts were vibrating at their natural frequencies, creating not noise but music.

Beautiful, chaotic, contradictory music.

The sound of an AuDHD life fully lived.

Chapter 15: Full Spectrum

"Why are you so public about it?" my dad asked, scrolling through my Instagram where I'd just posted a video of myself stimming while explaining executive dysfunction. "You could just... live your life quietly."

"Because quiet is how we disappeared for generations," I told him. "Quiet is how kids like me grow up thinking they're broken. Quiet is compliance, and compliance nearly killed me."

Living openly as AuDHD wasn't just a personal choice. It was a political act.

The Visibility Decision

The decision to be publicly, unapologetically, visibly neurodivergent came gradually, then all at once.

Gradually, as I tested the waters with small disclosures. All at once, the day I decided that hiding was more exhausting than any consequence of visibility could be.

I changed my bio on all platforms: "Actually AuDHD. Actually okay with it."

I started posting the reality, not just the highlights:

- Videos of me stimming during work
- Photos of my accommodation tools
- Stories about executive dysfunction
- Celebrating "minor" achievements like successful phone calls
- Meltdown recovery in real-time
- The chaos and beauty of special interests

"You're making yourself unemployable," a well-meaning friend warned.

"I'm making myself honestly employable," I corrected. "Anyone who wouldn't hire me because I'm openly neurodivergent isn't someone I want to work for anyway."

The Both/And Philosophy

The pushback came from unexpected places. Not just from neurotypicals who thought I should hide, but from within the neurodivergent community itself.

"You're too high-functioning to really understand autism," someone commented.

"You're too visibly struggling to represent ADHD positively," said another.

"Pick a lane," demanded the algorithms and the advocacy groups and the people who needed simple narratives.

But I was both/and, not either/or.

I was capable of brilliant work AND sometimes couldn't remember to shower. I was articulate in writing AND sometimes went nonverbal. I needed support AND lived independently. I was disabled AND capable. I was struggling AND thriving.

"Your existence confuses people," my therapist observed.

"Good," I said. "Confusion leads to questions. Questions lead to understanding. Understanding leads to acceptance."

I refused to be palatable. To minimize either my struggles or my strengths to fit someone else's narrative about what neurodivergence should look like.

The Ripple Effects

The visibility created ripples I hadn't anticipated.

Former classmates reached out: "This explains so much about me."

Parents of newly diagnosed kids: "Seeing you live successfully gives me hope."

Employers: "We want to hire more neurodivergent people but don't know how."

Other late-diagnosed adults: "I thought I was alone."

Each message reinforced that visibility mattered. That representation mattered. That living openly wasn't just about me – it was about every undiagnosed kid staring at their ceiling at 3 AM wondering why they couldn't be normal.

I started mentoring, formally and informally. Coffee meetings with newly diagnosed adults. Zoom calls with parents. Consulting with companies on neuroinclusion. Speaking at conferences where I stimmed on stage and nobody died.

"You're becoming the representation you needed," Jordan said.

"We all are," I reminded her. Because it wasn't just me. It was a movement of neurodivergent people refusing to hide anymore.

The Systemic Challenges

Living openly also meant confronting systems that weren't built for us.

Healthcare that pathologized our existence. Education that punished our learning styles. Employment that demanded neurotypical performance. Social structures that excluded us by design.

I became fluent in bureaucracy, learning to navigate systems while advocating for change. Writing letters to insurance companies explaining why noise-canceling headphones were medical equipment. Fighting with HR departments about accommodation requests. Educating medical professionals about adult presentation of AuDHD.

"You shouldn't have to fight this hard to exist," Alex said, watching me draft my third appeal letter that week.

"No," I agreed. "But if I don't fight, the next person has to fight just as hard. Maybe if I fight loud enough, they won't have to."

The Community Building

I started organizing. First online, then in person.

Monthly neurodivergent meetups in sensory-friendly spaces. Skill-shares where we taught each other our coping strategies. Support groups for specific challenges. Celebration parties for achievements neurotypicals wouldn't understand.

We created resource lists: neurodivergent-friendly doctors, therapists, employers, spaces. We shared scripts for difficult conversations, templates for accommodation requests, strategies for system navigation.

"You're building an entire parallel support structure," my sister observed, helping me set up for another meetup.

"We're building the structure that should have existed all along," I corrected.

The community grew. What started as five people in my living room became fifty people in rented spaces. Online groups with thousands of members. Connections across cities, countries, continents.

We weren't just supporting each other. We were changing the conversation about neurodivergence.

The Future Generation Focus

The messages that mattered most came from young people.

Teenagers who saw my content and recognized themselves. College students who learned to advocate because they saw it was possible. Kids who stimmed freely because they saw adults doing it.

"My daughter watches your videos," a parent told me. "She's eight and AuDHD. Seeing you makes her believe she can have a future."

That broke me. In the best way.

I started creating content specifically for young neurodivergent people. Not inspiration porn about "overcoming" neurodivergence, but real talk about living with it. The good, the bad, the complicated. The both/and of it all.

I talked about:

- Choosing careers that work with your brain
- Building relationships as your authentic self
- Managing burnout and preventing it
- The dignity of needing support
- The power of community
- The importance of accommodation, not adaptation

"You make it look easy," a teenager messaged me.

"I make it look possible," I corrected. "It's never easy. But it's possible, and it's worth it, and you deserve to exist as you are."

The Integration of Everything

119

Three years into living openly as AuDHD, I'd built a life that would have been unimaginable during my masked years.

A career that utilized my pattern recognition and creative chaos. Relationships based on authentic connection. A home designed for my sensory needs. A schedule that worked with my executive function. A community that understood and celebrated neurodivergence.

Was it perfect? No. I still had meltdowns, shutdowns, burnout cycles. Still fought with insurance companies and struggled with phone calls and forgot to eat when hyperfocused.

But it was real. It was mine. It was sustainable in a way masking had never been.

"You're different," my mom said, but this time it wasn't worried or confused. It was proud.

"I'm the same person I've always been," I told her. "I'm just not hiding it anymore."

The Manifesto Moment

At a neurodiversity conference, speaking to a room full of people whose brains worked in beautiful, chaotic, different ways, I said what I'd been building toward:

"We don't need to be fixed. We need to be accommodated. We don't need to be normal. We need to be accepted. We don't need to overcome our neurodivergence. We need to overcome the systems that disable us. We are not broken. We are not less than. We are not inspiration or tragedy. We are human beings with different operating systems, deserving of dignity, respect, and the right to exist as we are. The problem was never us. The problem was always a world that demanded one way of being. We are the full spectrum of human neurology, and we will no longer shrink ourselves to fit into neurotypical boxes. This is what AuDHD looks like. This is what neurodivergence looks like. Complicated. Contradictory. Beautiful. Real. Both/and, not either/or. All of it, all at once, all valid."

The room erupted. Flapping, rocking, bouncing, vocal stimming – a symphony of neurodivergent joy that would have horrified neurotypical observers but was the most beautiful sound I'd ever heard.

The Hope and the Hard

Living openly wasn't utopian. There were real consequences.

Lost opportunities from discriminatory employers. Ended friendships with people who couldn't accept the real me. Family members who remained uncomfortable. Online harassment from people who thought neurodivergence was trendy or fake or attention-seeking.

But for every loss, there were gains. For every closed door, windows opened. For every person who couldn't accept me, three more found permission to accept themselves.

"Was it worth it?" my therapist asked during what would be our final session – not because I was "cured" but because I'd learned to be my own advocate.

"Every single consequence," I said. "Every lost opportunity, every ended relationship, every hard conversation. Worth it to be real. Worth it to help others be real. Worth it to exist as I actually am."

The Continuing Symphony

The journey wasn't over. Would never be over. There was no "cured" or "fixed" or "normal" waiting at the end. Just continued understanding, continued advocacy, continued existence as my full, complicated, beautiful AuDHD self.

But now I wasn't alone. We weren't alone. A whole community of us, living openly, supporting each other, changing the world one unmasked day at a time.

The full spectrum wasn't just about autism or ADHD. It was about the full spectrum of human neurology, the full spectrum of ways to be human, the full spectrum of possibility when we stop demanding everyone tune to the same frequency.

We were not broken radios needing repair.

We were an orchestra, each playing our own frequency, creating a symphony that neurotypical ears were finally starting to hear.

And we were just getting started.

Epilogue: The Remix

I'm thirty-two now. Five years into knowing I'm AuDHD. Five years of unmasking, rebuilding, discovering who I actually am underneath twenty-seven years of performance.

My apartment is a testament to accommodation without apology. Fairy lights instead of overhead bulbs. A pacing path worn into the carpet. Whiteboards covering entire walls with color-coded systems that I follow religiously until I don't. Noise-canceling headphones in every room. A freezer full of exactly three safe foods bought in bulk. It looks like chaos to neurotypical eyes, but it's my chaos, designed for my brain.

I'm writing this at 4:17 AM because that's when my brain decided words were happening. My coffee is in the wrong mug because I forgot to run the dishwasher, and that small wrongness is bothering me enough that I've mentioned it here, but not enough to stop writing to fix it. Classic AuDHD – simultaneously hyperfocused and distracted, bothered and coping.

If I'd Known Then

People ask what would have been different if I'd been diagnosed as a child. It's a question that used to send me spiraling into grief. Now it just makes me thoughtful.

Would I have avoided the burnout cycles? Maybe. Would I have struggled less with relationships? Possibly. Would I have made different career choices? Probably.

But also: Would I have developed the same resilience? Would I have learned to study my own mind with scientific precision? Would I have found the same fierce self-advocacy? Would I have the same deep empathy for others struggling without words for their experience?

There's no control group for a life. No way to A/B test existence. The path I took – through confusion, masking, burnout, and finally understanding – is the only path I have.

"I wish I'd known sooner," a newly diagnosed forty-five-year-old tells me at a support group.

"Me too," I say. "But we know now. And now is when we have."

To the Undiagnosed

If you're reading this and seeing yourself, if your heart is racing with recognition, if you're thinking "but I can't be AuDHD because..." – stop.

You can be AuDHD and successful. You can be AuDHD and struggling. You can be AuDHD and married, single, parent, child, professional, unemployed, verbose, nonverbal, social, isolated. You can be AuDHD and not fit any stereotype or every stereotype or contradictory stereotypes simultaneously.

AuDHD doesn't have a look. It has a feeling. The feeling of your brain being at war with itself. The feeling of being too much and not enough. The feeling of exhaustion from existing in a world built for different brains.

If you recognize that feeling, seek evaluation. Find community. Start unmasking in whatever tiny ways feel safe. Learn your patterns. Honor your needs. Stop apologizing for your existence.

You're not broken. You're not lazy. You're not too sensitive or not sensitive enough. You're not failing at being human.

You're neurodivergent in a neurotypical world, and that's hard. It's okay that it's hard. It's not your fault that it's hard.

The Vision Forward

I dream of a world where neurodivergent kids grow up knowing exactly how their brains work. Where accommodation is automatic, not fought for. Where stimming is as unremarkable as breathing. Where different ways of communicating, learning, working, and existing are valued equally.

I dream of education that adapts to different brains instead of demanding all brains adapt to it. Workplaces with sensory rooms and flexible schedules and communication preferences. Healthcare that treats neurodivergence as a difference, not a deficit. Architecture designed for sensory diversity. Technology that supports executive dysfunction. Communities built on acceptance of all neurotypes.

It sounds utopian. Impossible. But every unmasked stim, every accommodation request, every openly neurodivergent person living their truth makes it a little more possible.

We're remixing what it means to be human. Expanding the definition. Making space for all the ways brains can be.

The Ongoing Journey

There's no end to this story because there's no end to being neurodivergent. No graduation from autism, no cure for ADHD, no final form where everything is figured out.

Every day is still a negotiation between my different needs. Every day still requires conscious effort to honor my neurodivergence instead of hiding it. Every day is still both/and – brilliant and struggling, capable and needing support, thriving and surviving.

But now I have words. Now I have community. Now I have understanding – of myself and from others. Now I have a life built for my actual brain instead of the brain I was pretending to have.

Some days are still hard. Meltdowns still happen. Executive dysfunction still strikes. Burnout still lurks. The world is still built for neurotypical brains, and that still causes daily friction.

But now I know why. Now I know it's not my fault. Now I know I'm not alone.

The Final Frequency

If you take nothing else from this story, take this:

Your brain is not wrong. Different is not less. Struggling doesn't mean failing. Needing support doesn't mean weak. Thinking differently doesn't mean thinking incorrectly.

You deserve to exist as you are. To stim freely. To honor your sensory needs. To communicate in ways that work for you. To build a life that fits your brain. To be accepted not despite your neurodivergence but including it.

The static you've been hearing isn't interference. It's your frequency trying to come through clearly. The push-pull isn't brokenness. It's complexity. The exhaustion isn't weakness. It's the natural result of living in a world not built for your brain.

You are not too much. You are not not enough. You are exactly who you're supposed to be, living in a world that hasn't caught up yet.

But we're changing that. One unmasked day at a time. One accommodation request at a time. One openly neurodivergent life at a time.

The remix isn't about becoming someone new. It's about uncovering who you've always been. It's about turning up your natural frequency and letting it play at full volume.

It's about being both/and in an either/or world and refusing to apologize for it.

My name is... well, my name doesn't matter. What matters is that I'm AuDHD. I'm thirty-two years old. I'm writing this at 4:43 AM while stimming and drinking coffee from the wrong mug. I'm successful and struggling. I'm thriving and surviving. I'm exactly who I'm supposed to be.

And so are you.

The music of our mixed frequencies might sound like chaos to some ears. But to those who understand, to those who share our neurotype, to those who've learned to listen – it's a symphony.

A beautiful, chaotic, contradictory symphony of human neurodiversity.

And we're just getting started.

[End]

The journey continues. The music plays on. The full spectrum of human neurology deserves to be seen, heard, understood, and celebrated.

Find your frequency. Turn up the volume. The world needs to hear your song.

Resources for AuDHD Adults

Note: All resources listed were active at time of publication. For updated links and additional resources, visit author website/resources

---

Diagnostic Tools and Screening Questionnaires

Autism Screening Tools (Free Online)

- **RAADS-R** (Ritvo Autism Asperger Diagnostic Scale-Revised)
    o embrace-autism.com/raads-r
    o Most comprehensive free autism screening tool
- **Autism Spectrum Quotient (AQ)**
    o psychology-tools.com/autism-spectrum-quotient
    o Quick 50-question screening
- **CAT-Q** (Camouflaging Autistic Traits Questionnaire)
    o embrace-autism.com/cat-q
    o Measures masking behaviors

ADHD Screening Tools (Free Online)

- **ASRS v1.1** (Adult ADHD Self-Report Scale)
    o psychology-tools.com/adult-adhd-self-report-scale
    o WHO-approved screening tool
- **DIVA-5** (Diagnostic Interview for ADHD in Adults)
    o divacenter.eu
    o Comprehensive self-assessment

Combined/Executive Function

- **BRIEF-A** (Behavior Rating Inventory of Executive Function-Adult)
  - Sample questions available through psychology practices
- **Conners Adult ADHD Rating Scales**
  - Information at mhs.com

AuDHD-Friendly Therapist Directories

Specialized Directories

- **Neurodivergent Therapist Directory**
  - ndtherapists.com
  - Therapists who are neurodivergent themselves
- **AANE Provider Directory**
  - aane.org/directory
  - Autism/neurodiversity-informed providers

General Directories with ND Filters

- **Psychology Today**
  - psychologytoday.com
  - Filter by: Autism, ADHD, Neurodiversity
- **TherapyDen**
  - therapyden.com
  - Strong neurodiversity-affirming filter options

Telehealth Options

- **Cerebral**
  - cerebral.com
  - ADHD-focused care
- **Done ADHD**
  - donefirst.com
  - ADHD assessment and treatment

Neurodivergent-Affirming Organizations

International Organizations

- **Autistic Self Advocacy Network (ASAN)**
  - autisticadvocacy.org
  - Run by and for autistic people
- **ADHD Foundation**
  - adhdfoundation.org.uk
  - Neurodiversity charity

U.S. Organizations

- **Asperger/Autism Network (AANE)**
  - aane.org
  - Support, education, and advocacy
- **Children and Adults with ADHD (CHADD)**
  - chadd.org
  - Largest ADHD organization

Women/Nonbinary Focused

- **Autism Women & Nonbinary Network**
  - awnnetwork.org
- **ADHD Women's Support Groups**
  - adhdwomen.org

BIPOC Neurodivergent Organizations

- **Black Women with ADHD**
  - blackwomenwithadhd.com
- **Autism in Black**
  - autisminblack.org

Recommended Books and Memoirs

AuDHD/Dual Diagnosis

- *"The ADHD Autism Connection"* by Diane Kennedy
- *"Divergent Mind"* by Jenara Nerenberg
- *"Is This Autism, ADHD, Both or Neither?"* by Meghan Ashburn

Autism Memoirs & Guides

- *"Unmasking Autism"* by Devon Price
- *"Odd Girl Out"* by Laura James
- *"Look Me in the Eye"* by John Elder Robison
- *"Nerdy, Shy, and Socially Inappropriate"* by Cynthia Kim

ADHD Books

- *"Driven to Distraction"* by Edward Hallowell
- *"You Mean I'm Not Lazy, Stupid or Crazy?!"* by Kate Kelly
- *"ADHD 2.0"* by Edward Hallowell & John Ratey
- *"A Radical Guide for Women with ADHD"* by Michelle Frank

Neurodiversity & Acceptance

- *"NeuroTribes"* by Steve Silberman
- *"The Power of Neurodiversity"* by Thomas Armstrong
- *"Authoring Autism"* by Melanie Yergeau

Online Communities and Support Groups

Reddit Communities

- r/AutisticWithADHD - Specifically for AuDHD
- r/aspergirls - Autism in women/femmes

- r/AutisticAdults - Adult autism community
- r/ADHD - General ADHD support
- r/adhdwomen - ADHD in women
- r/neurodiversity - Broader neurodivergent community

Discord Servers

- **Neurodivergent Universe** - Mixed neurotypes welcome
- **AuDHD Adults** - Combination autism/ADHD focus
- **Actually Autistic** - Autism-focused server

Facebook Groups

- Autistic Women & Nonbinary Network
- ADHD Women's Super Support Group
- AuDHD Support Group
- Neurodivergent Cleaning Crew
- Executive Dysfunction Meals

Other Platforms

- **Wrong Planet** - wrongplanet.net
  - Long-standing autism community forum
- **ADHD Forums** - adhd-community.org
  - Moderated support forums

Workplace Accommodation Resources

Know Your Rights

- **Job Accommodation Network (JAN)**
  - askjan.org
  - Free, confidential accommodation guidance
- **U.S. EEOC (Equal Employment Opportunity Commission)**
  - eeoc.gov/disability-discrimination
  - Legal rights and protections

Accommodation Ideas & Templates

- **Workplace Accommodations for ADHD**
  - chadd.org/workplace
- **Autism @ Work Playbook**
  - disabilityin.org/autism-playbook

Remote Work Resources

- **We Work Remotely**
  - weworkremotely.com
  - Remote-first job board
- **FlexJobs**
  - flexjobs.com
  - Flexible and remote positions

Self-Employment Resources

- **Freelancers Union**
  - freelancersunion.org
- **Neurodivergent Entrepreneurs Facebook Group**

Sensory-Friendly Product Recommendations

Noise Management

- **Loop Earplugs** - Discrete noise reduction
- **Flare Calmer** - Reduces harsh frequencies
- **Bose QuietComfort** - Noise-canceling headphones
- **Brown/White Noise Apps** - Brain.fm, Noisli

Light Sensitivity

- **TheraSpecs** - Migraine/light sensitivity glasses
- **Flux** - Computer blue light filter (free)
- **Philips Hue** - Adjustable color/brightness bulbs
- **Blackout curtains** - Various brands

Fidget/Stim Tools

- **Stimagz** - Magnetic fidget toys
- **Chewelry** - Chewable jewelry for oral stims
- **Thinking Putty** - Quiet fidget option
- **Tangle Toys** - Classic fidget toy

Weighted/Compression

- **Gravity Blanket** - Weighted blankets
- **Comfylids** - Weighted eye masks
- **Compression clothing** - Various athletic brands
- **Weighted lap pads** - Portable option

Organization/Executive Function

- **Tile Trackers** - Find lost items
- **Time Timer** - Visual time management
- **Notion** - Free organization app
- **Goblin Tools** - AI task breakdown app
- **How to ADHD YouTube Channel** - Free strategies

Comfort Items

- **Seamless socks** - SmartKnitKids (adult sizes too)
- **Tagless clothing** - Various brands
- **Squishmallows** - Comfort plushies
- **Adult weighted stuffed animals** - Various brands

Crisis Resources

Mental Health Crisis

- **988** - Suicide & Crisis Lifeline (U.S.)
- **Crisis Text Line** - Text HOME to 741741
- **International Crisis Lines** - findahelpline.com

Autism/ND Specific Crisis Support

- **Autism Crisis Support** - autismcrisisupport.org
- **ASAN Crisis Resources** - autisticadvocacy.org/crisis

Additional Resources

Podcasts

- *ADHD for Smart Ass Women*
- *Neurodivergent Moments*
- *Spectrumly Speaking*
- *The Neurodiversity Podcast*

YouTube Channels

- How to ADHD
- Yo Samdy Sam
- Paige Layle
- Connor DeWolfe

Mobile Apps

- **Routinery** - Routine management
- **Tiimo** - Visual daily planner
- **Breathwrk** - Anxiety/meltdown management
- **Sanvello** - Mood tracking

References

1. **Adler, L. A., Spencer, T. J., & Wilens, T. E. (Eds.). (2015).** Attention-deficit hyperactivity disorder in adults and children. Cambridge University Press.

2. **Amaze. (2018).** Inclusive education for students on the autism spectrum. Amaze.

3. **Bargiela, S., Steward, R., & Mandy, W. (2016).** The experiences of late-diagnosed women with autism spectrum conditions: An investigation of the female autism phenotype. Journal of Autism and Developmental Disorders, 46(10), 3281-3294.

4. **Baron-Cohen, S. (2008).** Autism and Asperger syndrome: The facts. Oxford University Press.

5. **Bottema-Beutel, K., Kapp, S. K., Lester, J. N., Sasson, N. J., & Hand, B. N. (2021).** Avoiding ableist language: Suggestions for autism researchers. Autism in Adulthood, 3(1), 18-29.

6. **Bury, S. M., Jellett, R., Spoor, J. R., & Hedley, D. (2023).** "It defines who I am" or "it's something I have": What language do [autistic] Australian adults [on the autism spectrum] prefer? Journal of Autism and Developmental Disorders, 53(2), 677-687.

7. **Cooper, K., Smith, L. G., & Russell, A. (2017).** Social identity, self-esteem, and mental health in autism. European Journal of Social Psychology, 47(7), 844-854.

8. **Crane, L., Batty, R., Adeyinka, H., Goddard, L., Henry, L. A., & Hill, E. L. (2018).** Autism diagnosis in the United Kingdom: Perspectives of autistic adults, parents and

professionals. Journal of Autism and Developmental Disorders, 48(11), 3761-3772.

9. **Fletcher-Watson, S., Adams, J., Brook, K., Charman, T., Crane, L., Cusack, J., Leekam, S., Milton, D., Parr, J. R., & Pellicano, E. (2019).** Making the future together: Shaping autism research through meaningful participation. Autism, 23(4), 943-953.

10. **Fuld, S. (2018).** Autism spectrum disorder: The impact of stressful and traumatic life events and implications for clinical practice. Clinical Social Work Journal, 46(3), 210-219.

11. **Huang, Y., Arnold, S. R., Foley, K. R., & Trollor, J. N. (2020).** Diagnosis of autism in adulthood: A scoping review. Autism, 24(6), 1311-1327.

12. **Jones, L., Goddard, L., Hill, E. L., Henry, L. A., & Crane, L. (2014).** Experiences of receiving a diagnosis of autism spectrum disorder: A survey of adults in the United Kingdom. Journal of Autism and Developmental Disorders, 44(12), 3033-3044.

13. **Jones, R. S., Quigney, C., & Huws, J. C. (2003).** First-hand accounts of sensory perceptual experiences in autism: A qualitative analysis. Journal of Intellectual & Developmental Disability, 28(2), 112-121.

14. **Kapp, S. K., Gillespie-Lynch, K., Sherman, L. E., & Hutman, T. (2013).** Deficit, difference, or both? Autism and neurodiversity. Developmental Psychology, 49(1), 59-71.

15. **Leadbitter, K., Buckle, K. L., Ellis, C., & Dekker, M. (2021).** Autistic self-advocacy and the neurodiversity movement: Implications for autism early intervention research and practice. Frontiers in Psychology, 12, 635690.

16. **Leedham, A., Thompson, A. R., Smith, R., & Freeth, M. (2020).** 'I was exhausted trying to figure it out': The

experiences of females receiving an autism diagnosis in middle to late adulthood. Autism, 24(1), 135-146.

17. **Lewis, L. F. (2017).** A mixed methods study of barriers to formal diagnosis of autism spectrum disorder in adults. Journal of Autism and Developmental Disorders, 47(8), 2410-2424.

18. **Milton, D., Ridout, S., Murray, D., Martin, N., & Mills, R. (2020).** The Participatory Autism Research Collective (PARC): Community views on the autism research agenda. University of Kent.

19. **Pellicano, E., & den Houting, J. (2022).** Annual research review: Shifting from 'normal science' to neurodiversity in autism science. Journal of Child Psychology and Psychiatry, 63(4), 381-396.

20. **Punshon, C., Skirrow, P., & Murphy, G. (2009).** The 'not guilty verdict': Psychological reactions to a diagnosis of Asperger syndrome in adulthood. Autism, 13(3), 265-283.

21. **Stagg, S. D., & Belcher, H. (2019).** Living with autism without knowing: Receiving a diagnosis in later life. Health Psychology and Behavioral Medicine, 7(1), 348-361.

22. **Tan, C. D. (2018).** "I'm a normal autistic person, not an abnormal neurotypical": Autism Spectrum Disorder diagnosis as biographical illumination. Social Science & Medicine, 197, 161-167.

www.ingramcontent.com/pod-product-compliance
Lightning Source LLC
Chambersburg PA
CBHW051718090426
42738CB00010B/1969